Foreword

All armies, whether it be due to necessity, curiosity, preference or mere opportunity, use weapons and equipment that are captured from the enemy. Arguably no other army in modern times, utilized captured foreign ordnance to such an extent as the Wehrmacht during World War II. It even went so far that these captured weapons and vehicles where assigned a Kenn nummer(identification numbers) by the Wehrmachts Waffenamt(German army's weapons department).

Germany is often praised for their great engineering and their greatness in design of weapons. The problem for Germany after WW1 was that in production they were utterly behind France and England at the time. The amount of private cars and trucks are one of the indicators of that.

There was lots of reasons why Germany lacked production capacity after the Great War, not only had it lost all its colonies, mainly to France and England, it had also been dismembered. Poland was again a free country, and Poland could produce to its own needs. Austria-Hungary was also dismembered, and broken up. The great weapons factories of Czechoslovakia was making weapons for the czechs themselves and exporting a great deal, instead of arming Austria and Germany.

Turkey(Ottoman empire) another Ally of Germany had also been broken up to bits. Again the main beneficiary being France and England, in dividing the land, colonies after the Great War.

All these colonies that went to France and England would later determine the other allies of the Great War Italy and Japan to react to what they saw as an unfair parting of the loot.

For this we must remember Charles De Gaulles words, "Nation States has no friends, Nation States have only lasting interests.". And probably his argument was why Franklin Delano Roosewelt did not recognise De Gaulle as a legitimate member of the negotiations at Yalta, for which Churchill and Stalin had recognized De Gaulle as the defacto leader of France in exile.

Another point about the Problems regarding German production was helped with the conquest of Northern France. The French industries was mobilized by the German occupant, as people needed jobs, and Germany needed production. Just before Barbarossa the Wehrmacht could field, 88 infantry divisions, 3 motorized infantry divisions and 1 Panzerdivision were largely equiped with French vehicles. Beside the captured vehicles, there were akso newly produced trucks. The main companies (Renault, Peugeot, Citroën, Panhard, Berliet and Saurer etc.) produced about 90000 new trucks for the German army between 1941 and 1944. Especially for the eastern front 200 French tanks were also converted to Mörserzugmittel and Artillerie-Schlepper and others to Bergepanzer or various tractors.

To note:
• Berliet :
Various Berliet trucks were used by the German army (DGRA, GDC, GDM, VDCA etc.) and about 30 Berliet tank carriers were used by the Wehrmacht.
During 1943-1944 for example, 1262 trucks (5t) were produced for the German army.

• Bernard :
A few Bernard trucks (fuel tank trucks etc.) were used by the German army.

• Citroën :
Many booty cars, trucks and halftracks (Citroën Kégresse P14, P17, P19) were captured and used by the Germans. The Citroën-Kégresse P19 = Ci380(f) can for example be found in the Schnelle Brigade West. Many other vehicles were produced for the Germans between 1941 and 1944 like for example :
- 3700 type 23 trucks
- 6000 type 32U trucks
- 15300 type 45 trucks (which was the majority of the trucks of Schnelle Brigade West)

• Delahaye :
About 1000 SdKfz-11 were produced for the Germans (ordered in 1942).
The Delahaye factory also produced spare parts for the Büssing-NAG 4500.

• ELMAG (in Mulhouse, Alsace) :
Production of 1143 SdKfz-8 halftracks and spare parts for German halftracks between 1942 and 1944.

• Ford :
At the beginning of WW2, the French Ford factories located at Poissy and Asnières were controlled by the Laffly company. They transformed 1000 Ford trucks into halftracked trucks (Maultier) and produced spare parts for the Ford trucks captured in Europe.

• Gnôme-Rhône :
Gnôme-Rhône in Gennevilliers (nowadays SNECMA) produced German engines for planes like the Henschel 129 and transport aircraft like the Messerschmitt Me 323.
Gnôme-Rhône motorcycles and side-cars were also used by the Germans.

• Hotchkiss :
During the occupation, Hotchkiss produced spare parts, engines and several chassis for the Germans from 1940 to 1944 . Some Laffly vehicles (R15R, S20TL, W15T etc.) and several Hotchkiss personnal cars (PKW Typ680, 686 and 686 PNA) were also produced for the Germans.

• Isobloc :

Numerous buses had been produced for the French army. Several W843M medical buses were used by the Germans. They could carry 30 lying wounded soldiers or a whole mobile chirurgical antenna.

• Laffly :

Many Laffly V15R, S15R, S20TL, W15T etc. were captured and used by the Germans.
A small number of armored SPW based on the W15T were produced for the Schnelle Brigade West.
In 1942, 60 Renault R-40 tanks were transformed for snow milling. 119 Renault R-40 were modified for the Luftwaffe (towing vehicles?) and 200 various German tracked vehicles were also modified for the Luftwaffe by the Laffly factory. Laffly transformed also 22 wheeled and 33 tracked vehicles in snowplough's.

• Latil :

Many Latil trucks and utility vehicles had been captured by the Wehrmacht. Some of the heavier trucks (Latil TAR H2) were again produced for the German forces.

• Lorraine :

Many Lorraine 37L and 38L were captured and used or modified by the Germans. The Lorraine factory also produced 500 SdKfz 9 in 1942.

• Matford (in Strasbourg, Alsace) :

Matford was born from the fusion between Ford and the French Mathis company. A few trucks were produced but mainly spare parts for the French booty Matford trucks like the Matford F917.
- F91A/92A car
- F91A type light truck
- V8-81
- F917-WS standard 4.5t truck
- F917-WS fuel tank truck

• Panhard & Levassor :

About 2000 Panhard trucks were delivered to the Germans army and about 1000 couples of tracks for the SdKfz-7 have been produced.

• Peugeot :
The factory is controlled by KDFWagen (future Volkswagen).
Many cars (Peugeot 202 and 402) and light trucks (Peugeot DMA, DK etc.) were captured and used but also produced. Between 1941 and 1944

Peugeot delivered the Germans :
- 12500 Peugeot DK5
- 15300 Peugeot DMA
- about 15000 Peugeot 202 and 402
That makes about 28000 trucks delivered to the Germans.
The factory produced also spare parts for the Kübelwagen and a few Volkswagen type 82 and 166 were completed. 150 SdKfz-10 per month were also planned to be produced in 1942 but the number delivered is unknown.

• Renault :
For Renault, most of the archives have disappeared during the allied bombings of 1944 but in François Vauvillier's book "l'automobile sous l'uniforme" it is indicated that about 28000 Renault trucks had been produced for the Germans during the occupation (AHS, AHN, AHR, AGC, ADK, ADH etc.). The Renault factories were administrated by Prinz Von Urach (who later became the press attaché of Daimler-Benz after WW2). About 23000 Renault AHS trucks were used by the Germans (booty and new produced ones).
For example, from 1941 to 1944, 4000 Renault AHN and 2000 Renault AHR had been produced for the German army. In 1943, 704 AGC3 were delivered.
Renault produced also spare parts for the SdKfz. 7 and SdKfz. 11.

• Saurer :
Several trucks were still produced for the Germans, especially the Saurer type 3CT which was well liked by the Wehrmacht. For example between 1943 and 1944 some 1800 3CT trucks were delivered to the Germans.

• Simca :

Simca produced personnal cars for the German/Italian Army 1941/1942: 5983 Simca 5 (aka Fiat 500 Topolino) and 3960 Simca 8 (aka Fiat 1100)
Production in 1943 was 122 Simca 8 and 19 Simca 5
In 1944 the production was 180 Simca 8 and 23 Simca 5

Simca was intended to produce 2500 SdKfz-2 Kettenkraftrad but there seem not to have been produced. Tracks for the SdKfz. 7, SdKfz. 10 and SdKfz.11 was also produced.

• Somua :
Beside the Somua S35 tanks, many MCL named S303(f) and MCG named S307(f) halftracks were captured. Some of these halfracks would be armored in Paris by Alfred Beckers workdetail.

• Talbot :
From 1941 to 1944, Talbot produced tracks for the SdKfz-7, SdKfz-10 and SdKfz-11, braces for the Büssing-NAG S4500 and complete steerings for the Panzer 38(t).

• Trippel :
The factory was located at Molsheim(Alsace) in the former Bugatti factory. They produced the Trippel SG6/41 amphibious car, the predecessor to the Schwimmwagen.

• UNIC :
About 200 UNIC TU1 U305(f) and 3000 UNIC P107 U304(f) were used by the German army.

© Dieter Almberger

• Willeme :
A few Willeme type DU10 (10t) heavy trucks were used by the German army.

Use of halftracks

Simplified overview indicating which vehicle is theoretically used to tow which gun, in the French army:

1) 25mm AT gun, 20-25mm AA guns etc.
• UNIC TU1 (25mm AT and wheeled supply trailer)
• Renault UE (25mm AT and tracked supply trailer)
• Latil M7T1 (25mm AT)
• Laffly V15T (25mm AT)
• Latil M7Z1 (25mm AA)

2) 47mm AT gun, 75mm field gun and 105mm C field gun
• Citroën-Kégresse P17
• UNIC P107
• Laffly S15T
• Laffly W15T

3) 105mm L and 155mm C field gun
• Citroën-Kégresse P14
• Somua MCG (4, 5 and 11)
• Laffly S25T
• Latil KTL4

4) 155mm GPF and GPFT
• Somua MCL (5 and 11)
• Laffly S35T (dedicated to the 155mm GPFT)

5) Various heavy artillery
• Older Panhard K13 and Renault EG still in service
• Latil TAR, TAR4, TAR5 and FTAR
• Laril TAR H2

CITROËN-KEGRESSE

The development of the light half-track vehicle goes back to the ideas of Adolphe Kégresse in 1910/1911, when, as a technical director of the vehicle fleet of the Russian czar Nicholas II, he had to deal with the off-road mobility of motor vehicles, especially in winter times. Kegresse obtained his patent for his half track system in 1913. While the concept of the tracked vehicle had been around since at least as early as the 1770s and half-tracked vehicles employing tracks composed of metal links had been designed and commercially-produced by shortly after the turn of the century, if not before. Kégresse was given the opportunity to put his design to practical use as the Technical Director of the motor pool of the Tsar of Russia from 1910-11. After returning to France due to the breakout of the Russian Revolution, Kégresse eventually formed a partnership with André Citroën and M. Hinstin and began perfecting the Kégresse Principle with Citroën in 1920. (Vauvillier, Boniface & Jeudy)

Kégresse was the first to successfully design a half-tracked chassis driven by a flexible band track which began as simple bands of rubber that were later reinforced with metal inserts. Another feature of the "Kégresse Principle" was a running gear composed of a large drive sprocket and idler, in-between which were typically 2 pairs of bogie wheels (each pair joined by suspension frame and both suspension frames held together by a suspension frame assembly) and one return roller on top of the suspension frame assembly. So the track system, which replaced the normal rear axle, had two endless rubber bands, which were later reinforced with metal inserts. The drive consisted of track and support rollers, a drive wheel and a deflection roller. The favorable ratio of chain support length/chain width resulted in a considerable improvement in off-road mobility.

Returning to France after the revolution in Russia, Kégresse looked for a financier to realize his ideas about the design of a half-track and found him in the industrialist M. Hinstin, who made it possible to let formulate Kégresse's ideas into reality.

From 1921, entrepreneur André Citroën placed the whole thing on a solid technical and financial basis. His Autochenille found imitators in many countries and admireres in many militaries. During the 1920's Citroen arrangenged many adventures or travels with the halftrack as its star, to show how good, tough and realiable the Citroen-Kegresse half track system was.

The half-track vehicles from Citroën were manufactured by the company "Citroën Département Autochenille", 159, Rue Armand Silvestre, Courbevoie, and came in larger numbers as a means of traction for the 7.5 cm artillery and as a transport vehicle for the motorized dragoons (voiture de dragons porté) were used in large numbers by the German Wehrmacht:

The first Citroën-Kégresse halftrack adopted by the French army was the P 7bis in 1928. At this time the French Army was in search of a fast vehicle that would be capable of towing the 75 mm model 1897 cannon cross-country and P 7bis was chosen. Only 6, according to most sources, were delivered to the Army. The P-7bis was extremely underpowered which severely limited its towing capacity and speed. The P 7bis was quickly replaced by the P 17, also produced by Citroën, which was an improvement but still underpowered and slow. (Vauvillier)

In 1925 the U.S. Army purchased two early 10 hp Citroën-Kégresse halftracks and in 1931 a P 17 was also purchased to evaluate them for possible adoption for use by the Army. While neither were chosen, because they were considered too small and underpowered, the influence of the Kégresse Principle is clearly seen in the running gear of the U.S. M series half-tracks (such as the M2A1) used by the U.S. Army prior to, during and after WW II. (Hunnicutt)

By 1934, in light of the impending introduction of rubber tires for artillery pieces, the French Army initiated a search for an improved towing vehicle for 75mm and also 105mm C guns. Several companies presented their vehicles for trials between the end of 1934 and 1936 but in the end the French Army chose two: the Citroën P 107 with Kégresse (half-track) drive and the Laffly S15 T with six-wheel drive. While the Laffly overall performed better, the Army chose both because the Laffly was more expensive and also because the production capacity of Laffly was more limited than Citroën. By September 1, 1939, there were about 1450 light artillery-towing vehicles on hand, of which approximately 1066 were Citroën/UNIC P 107s. (Vauvillier)

By 1934 Citroën was in financial trouble and the company was taken over by the Michelin brothers. In 1935 André Citroën died of cancer. The Michelin brothers decided to focus on large-scale production items and thus sold off the licensing of the specialized vehicles. S.A. des Automobiles UNIC bought the rights to the P 107 and production began at their factory in Puteaux in 1937. By the time the war commenced, the majority of the P 107s in the French arsenal had been produced by UNIC . The only Citroën halftrack that continued in production after 1935 was the P 107 (other than the P 19, which continued to be produced by Chenard & Walcker), but other Citroën vehicles that were already in use by the French army were captured and utilized by the Germans. The following are the three mentioned by Spielberger (Pg. 57) with the German designation in brackets:
The P 14 [Ci 306 (f)], as the tower for the heavy artillery. According to Vauvillier Citroën produced only 52 examples of this vehicle.

The P 17 [Ci 301 (f)], as tower for the 7,5 cm leFK 97. According to Vauvillier 1142 were produced before production ceased. The following photo shows a P 17 in French service in a parade in 1939 towing the 75mm:

The P 19 [Ci 380 (f)], Personnel Carrier for the Motorized Infantry. There were at least around 600 of these in the French Army by 1939 (I was unable to determine if this number refers only to the P 19B or to all versions of it). - Transportkraftwagen Ci 380 (f) for motorized dragoons.

In the extensive production program for half-track vehicles, Citroën offered the following types, also commercially available:

Details in () for bore/stroke in mm.
- P 15 NB, 6 cylinder (72x100)
- P 15 N, 6 cylinder (80x100) P. 26 B, 6 cylinder (75x100)
- P 28, 6 cylinder (80x100)
- P. 104, 6 - Cylinder (80x100)
- P. 17 E, 4-cylinder (75x100)
- P. 19 B, 6-cylinder (72x100)
- P. 14 B, 6-cylinder (75x100)
-P. 107 as a tractor for the 7.5cm Anti tank gun.

Being produced during more than 5 years, the P17 goes through an evolution, starting with the

P17A (hardly an official name) and P17B. Though principally based on C4, these models are built on the chassis of the B15, a truck derivate of the B14. Weight of chassis (no carrosserie, empty car): 1200 kgs.

The P17C appears in 1932, now with the engine of the C4G: 1767 cm3 (75x100). This is probably also the stage when the P17s gets a new chassis, designed for the purpose: It's flat (without the slung shape at the rear) and the empty car weight is increased to 1470 kgs without body.

The P17C is followed by P17D and P17E, with minor modifications.

The P17 is a light Kegresse and by far the model with the highest production numbers. Somewhere it is said that for the French army alone more than 1700 cars were delivered and surely Citroën supplied the armies in other countries as well. But the P17 model was also applied in other areas such as agriculture and forestry and public service

When Citroën stopped producing suitable chassis for half-track vehicles in the mid-1930s, the P. 107 was the only one that UNIC took over and continued to build.

P19 vehicles were prepared as personnel carriers and commUNIC ations vehicles for the Schnelle Brigade West.

French Half-track with the Flieger Bergungstrupp(Aircraft salvage unit)

CITROËN-KEGRESSE P 14

NUMBER OF COPIES 52
Existing September 1, 1939

The principle of counter-support traction, i.e. in a semi-trailer on a fifth wheel pivot, a system offering numerous technical advantages (resistance to wear due to friction, smaller turning radius, better stability of part), was tested for the first time on the Citroën Kégresse P 16, intended for the 155 CS. This 1929 prototype, which "is not the definitive model planned by Citroën", has a 4-cylinder 15hp engine, intended to be replaced by a 6-cylinder 14hp engine giving much greater brake power. On May 23, 1929, Vincennes considered that "the assembly formed by the Citroën-Kégresse tractor and the 155CS cannon on a running gear is of real interest for the motorization of the army".

Designated P 14, the series tractor was released in 1930 and 1931 in around sixty units, with bodywork as a piece tractor with counter-support, but also as a van (in fact a station wagon with a fixed roof and side curtains) with two bench seats for the transport of 9 servants and the traction of the box-trailer.

Lemberg is what today is known as Lviv, then part of Poland(Know as Lwow), now Ukraine

Displacement: 6 cyl., 2,655 cc
Max power: 42 hp at 2,800 rpm
Number of gears: 2x (3+ rear) Length:4,87 m
Empty weight: approx. 3,600 kg Width:1.75 m
Payload: approx. 1,700 kg
Max. speed:25 km/h

Wheelbase: 2.70m

Pic
Standard P 14 part tractor, N° 78 051, with torpedo cab, while the P 16 prototype had a panel cab. Here, the 155 CS is not on its running gear, which is normal for evolution in all terrain.

CITROËN-KEGRESSE P17

A light artillery tractor

Nunmber produced 1 442

Put into service in 1928 by the French army, the Citroën-Kégresse P 7bis (16 examples with a 20 hp B2 engine) demonstrated their remarkable tactical mobility linked to the low unit pressure of their tracks, their low relief and their ease of driving. For towed equipment, 75 mm model 1897 or box, the undercarriage system (p. 124 and photo p. 159), also signed by Citroën-Kégresse, proves to be an excellent solution. The experiment was a success and, in 1929, 214 Citroën-Kégresse light tractors of a new model equipped with the 30 hp C4 engine were ordered. This first order concerns the P 10 type, which will actually be delivered under the designation of P17A (CHD type engine, 4 cylinders 72 x 100). Successive versions will see the light of day, up to the P17E (engine type P 34, 4 cylinders 75 x 100) slightly more powerful. In total, approximately 1,500 copies, to be delivered over several annual years.

Citroën-Kégresse Artillerieschlepper P17

While we are not yet in the period of rearmament, the importance of these orders is explained by the organization of the 75mm light artillery regiment with all-terrain tractors defined in 1929:

-to each battery (4 pieces), 4 piece tractors, 6 box tractors, 1 MT light trailer tractor (p. 123); -at the staff of each group (with 3 batteries), 4 MT heavy trailer tractors:

On mobilization, the French army listed 1,442 Citroën Kégresse P 17s in service. Those that we were able to gradually withdraw service as field artillery regiments thanks to the arrival of the P107 and where temporarily assigned to the traction of the 47 anti-tank model 1937 in the automobile units (decision of June 3, 1937) and a little later to the traction of light anti-aircraft pieces of 25 mm model 1938 and 1939, pending the release, or so it was hoped, of the new fast tractors with special bodywork from the 1937 program.

In the heat of May-June 1940, the Citroën-Kégresses showed their age and their insufficient performance: "the equipment is too slow, so that during each stall, or each stage, each anti-tank section, after having delayed the unit of the point of support of which it formed part, was, after a short time, far in the rear and most often uncovered. The best equipment for this period would have been the 47 self-propelled gun. »> (Lt Millot, commander of the all-terrain tractor BDAC of the 3rd DLM, from June 9 to 25, report of October 17, 1940).

Apart from speed, the artillery also needed a more powerful tractor (capable of towing the 105mm Cannon weighing 1.7 t), capable of transporting 5 men with their equipment and ammunition. Several prototypes, including the Latil M2 TL 6 (p. 224), presented themselves in this capacity at Vincennes between the end of 1934 and 1936; only two will be retained:

- the Citroën P107 tractor with a Kégresse track;
- the Laffly S15 T six-wheel-drive tractor.

The second is watched with particular interest, especially for the artillery of cavalry divisions, "because of the known disadvantages of the track for light artillery tractors called to travel on the road at least as much as in varied terrain . (June 18, 1936).

On the other hand, the new P107 half-track was not without advantages: it was cheaper to produce, it could be mass-produced, whereas Laffly's industrial capacities always would remain limited.

These two photos, taken at the end of May 1940 a few seconds apart by two different operators, show the same vehicle, N° 82 546, in one of the emergency jobs devolved to the P 17 during the campaign: the traction of the cannon 47 anti-tank, here fitted with RAF Beaufils system wheels in cast aluminum alloy, derived from a model 1937. The three-quarter front view, showing the emergency mounting of the spare wheel on the front left, is to our knowledge unprecedented.

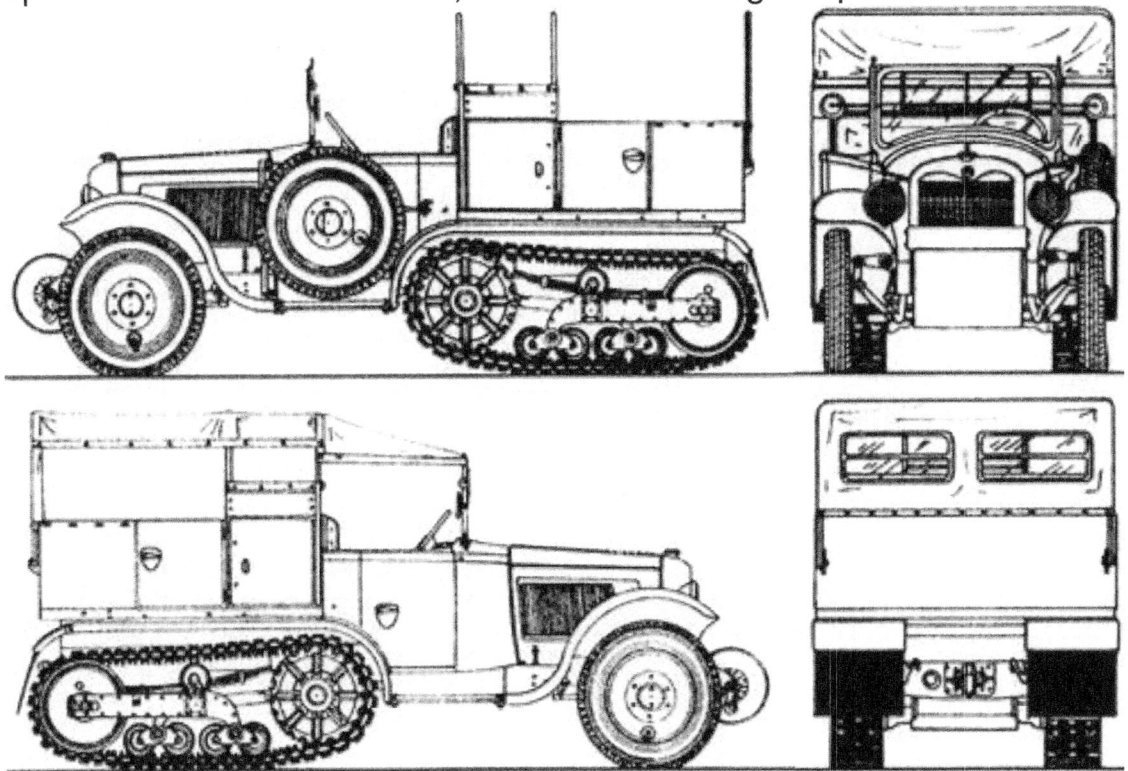

Number of cylinders: 4
Displacement: 1,625 cc (P 17A)
Displacement: 1,770 cc (P 17E)
Max Power: 30 to 31.5 hp at 2,800 rpm
Gears: 2x (3+ reverse)

Payload:1850 kg
Towed load:1 300 kg
Wheelbase: 2,50 m
Front track: 1,23 m
Rear track: 1,23 m
Lenght:4,38 m
Width: 1,69 m
Height (hood): 2,09 m
Max speed: 28 km/h (P 17A)
32 km/h (P 17E)

Citroen Kegresse in German service with a Farman French bomber in the hangar

CITROËN-KEGRESSE P 19

Citroen-Kegress P19, Dragoon car, for 7 men

This famous half-tracked car was an initial, imperfect response to the conditions required in 1928-1929 for mounted dragoons: sufficiently fast movement on the road and in varied terrain, extended means of action, great maneuverability, low visibility, and driving as easy as possible. Four distinct versions will be put into service:

- rifle-scout car (or FM24/29 LMG squad): two side benches facing each other at the rear, paneled chests at the front for personnel haversacks plus 4 special FM24/29 LMG haversacks. The platoon is 7 cars (3 groups of 2 cars carrying 6 men and 1 FM24/29 LMG, plus a platoon leader car with 7 men).

-machine gun car: very different from the old layout adopted on the C4 P10 and P 17, the body of the C6 P19 machine gun car is built on the same plan as the scout car: two seats and trunks in the front. The platoon is 5 cars (4 machine guns each carrying 6 men, 1 platoon leader with 7 men).

- mortar car: externally identical to the machine-gun car, it only differs in the arrangement of the chests receiving the dismantled 81 mm Brandt mortar and 54 shells. Platoons of 5 cars (4 mortar to 7 men, 1 platoon leader to 7 men).

- anti-tank gun car: a particular type of car, called P 19BT (T for tractor) was adopted to tow, first the 37 mm gun, then the 25 mm AC model 1934. The P 19BT has a higher gear ratio which reduced its top speed to 32 km/h. A tactically much more satisfactory solution will be found by in 1937: instead of being towed, the 25 mm cannon is carried, barrel forward, by a system of rails also allowing it to fire on board the vehicle. . The cannon group (two pieces) is two cars, 2 trucks and a trailer.

In the organization of the 1932 type cavalry division, each of the five BDPs has 99 all-terrain cars, distributed as follows: -11 cars (squadron leader, command platoon, and 5 cars for the off-road rank).

-32 cars to each of the two rifle squadrons (command platoon, 3 rifle platoons, 1 machine-gun platoon, 1 60 mm mortar piece):

24 cars to machine gun squadron and gear (command platoon, 2 machine gun platoons, 1 81mm mortar platoon, 2 groups of 25mm guns).

On mobilization, there were 547 P 19 dragoon-type cars, some of which, from the 1st and 4th RDP, finally complete on six-wheeled vehicles, were reassigned in the winter of 1939-1940. Most of the CK P 19 carried out the May-June campaign within the light cavalry divisions. Three of these regiments (with 2 battalions including 1 on vans), the 2nd, 3rd and 5th RDP assigned to the 3rd, 2nd and 1st DLC, come from the transformation of the old BDP of the same number. The 14 and 15° RDP (4 and 5 DLC), coming from the general reserve, are organized on the same type.

Zugkraftwagen Ci/380(f) (Citroën-Kégresse P19)

Different body versions of the P 19were offered - most P19s were used by the armies of. France, Belgium, Poland.

Deadweight: 2 200 kg
Payload: 700 kg
Rayon d'action: 350 km
Max speed: 46 km/h

CITROËN-KEGRESSE P 19B

Citroën-Kégresse P19B (CK P19B) (Chenard et Walcke VLTT)
The French army used about 600 of these as liaison halftracks in 1939.

P19B from 1931 was 11cm wider and heavier: 1620 kg.
Compared to the P17 the tracks are the same length and type, but the diameter of the front pulley was larger and the rear pulley smaller. The P19 can also be recognized by the bonnet.

Citroën-Kégresse with 4 seats and 6 seats of the successive types P 10, P 17 then P 19 were the subject of orders. In the french army the P19 was used as a 6-seater all-terrain liaison car.

As stated the P19B (6-cylinder, engine) came in 1931 and would still be widely in service in 1939, with several hundred examples (estimate, around 600). In 1938, Chenard & Walcker ensured the manufacture of a market-probably the last of 68 P19B, plus a car identified under the name of P19D, equipped, for possible mobilization orders, with the new Citroën 4-cylinder, 78x100 Traction

11hp engine. It was tested in the autumn of 1938, the prototype P19D was satisfactory (lower petrol consumption for a similar performance) but its mass production was not undertaken because the Kégresse was too slow ub convoys of modern vehicles, while towing artillery.

After Citroen filed for bankruptcy and was taken over by the Michelin brothers in 1935, the production of half-tracks was no longer ensured by the Quai de Javel. To honor current contracts, Kégresse manufacturing was continued at UNIC (P107 light artillery tractors) and Chenard-Walcker (VLTT, the name by Chenard-Walcker).

Number of cylinders: 6
Displacement: 2,442 cm3
Max power: 42 hp at 2,800 rpm
Payload: 650 kg
Wheelbase: 2,60 m
Length:4,70 m
Width : 1.70m
Number of gears: 3+ reverse
Weight: 2,230 kg
Maximum speed : 52 km/h(6 cylinders, 42hp at 2800 rpm)
Weight : 2.23t (live load 0.65t)

SOMUA

SOMUA is an abbreviation for Société d'Outillage Mécanique et d'Usinage d'Artillerie (Somua), Saint Quen (Seine), meaning something like Mechanical Tools and Artillery Machining Company (Somua), Saint Quen (Seine).

In 1912, the French company "La Société Motoculture Française SA" in Paris obtained the Meyenburg Bodenfräsen manufacturing rights for France, Spain and Argentina. A prototype was demonstrated at a show at the agricultural school in Grignon near Seine et Oise on 16th October 1913. In 1919, these manufacturing rights were taken over by the company SOMUA (Société d'Outillage Mécanique et d'Usinage d'Artillerie) at 170, Boulevard Victor-Hugo in Saint-Ouen, France. Although SOMUA had been founded in 1835, it took until 1914 to take over the activities of three companies, the Usines Bouhey and the Ets. Farcot, both well-known general engineers and constructors of heavy military equipment, and the automobile construction division of the Société Schneider. The main activity of the new group would remain the production of commercial vehicles, making good use of the fame the Schneider trucks and buses had already established for themselves. During World War I SOMUA became famous for their artillery tractors and tanks.

The history of SOMUA trucks ended in 1955, when they amalgamated with the companies Latil, Floirat and the Renault trucks division to form SAVIEM (Société Anonyme de Véhicules Industriels et Equipements Mécaniques). In 1962 SOMUA dealt a fusion with Henri Ernault (lathes constructor) in Paris. H. Ernault SOMUA was formed, resulting in more than 60,000 machines working all over the world. The SOMUA name still survives in the lathes construction of SOMUA Montzeron.

As SOMUA had made a name for themselves during the Great War, Somua comtinued to deliver vehicles to the French Army during the prewar and up til World War 2. Reduced production continued during the German occupation.

Some of the products in the SOMUA line was customary trucks with the payload classes from 3.5 to 10 t, also with special bodies, mUNIC ipal and fire-fighting vehicles.

Somua used two basic petrol engines in the 1930's. 4 and 6 cylinder engines with 100 mm bore and 150 mm stroke and a 6-cylinder with 115 mm bore and 150 mm stroke. Optionally, the vehicles could also be equipped with diesel engines. The carburettor engines also drove the bulk of the half-track vehicles.

As early as the late 1920s, SOMUA was supplying half-track vehicles based on the Kégresse-Hinstin half track system to the French army, but also to private customers. Two basic models with a number of technical modifications were offered, the MCG and MCL models.

aThe French army used 345 Somua MCG5 to tow the 105mm L Mle1936 Schneider guns and caissons, 315 SOMUA MCG4 and MCG11 to to tow the 155mm C Mle1917 Schneider guns and 312 SOMUA MCG5 to tow the caissons of the 155mm C Mle1917 Schneider guns.There was also about 440 Somua MCG4 and MCG5 recovery tractors (theoretically 1 for each 47mm AT gun, 75mm Mle1897 field gun, 105mm L Mle1936 and 155mm C Mle1917 battery as well as 3 for each light tank battalion).

There are aslo 24 SOMUA MCG 4 halftracks in the French navy to tow 8 155mm L Mle1932 Schneider guns (3 per gun). There is therefore a total of about 1436 SOMUA MCG tractors used by the French troops in 1940.

Concerning the 105mm L Mle1936 gun was arranged in two vehicle teams. A first SOMUA MCG towed the gun and carried 28 shells. A second SOMUA MCG carried the crew of the gun (8 men), various equipment and it towed a Mle1939 SOMUA trailer with 64 shells. The second Somua MCG instead of the crew could carry 28 additional shells (if the crew was transported in other vehicles). Each 105mm L Mle1936 had therefore 92-105 shells immediately available.

Concerning the 155mm C Mle1917 gun was arranged in two vehicle teams. A first Somua MCG and towed the gun and carried 12 shells. A second Somua MCG carried the crew of the gun (8 men), various equipment towed a Mle1935 Somua trailer with 34 shells. The second Somua MCG instead of the crew could carry 20 additional shells (if the crew was transported in other vehicles). Each 155mm C Mle1917 had therefore 46-66 shells immediately available.

In French service the SOMUA MCG specification was
Weight: 4.92t for the tractor and 6.8t for the standard halftrack (live load 1.5t + towed load 3.5t)
Length: 5.20m for the tractor and 5.30m for the standard halftrack
Width: 2.17m
Height: 2.60m for the tractor and 2.85m for the standard halftrack
Max speed: 31 km/h (4 cylinders, 4712cm3, 55hp for MCG4 and 60hp for MCG5 and MCG11)

here a picture with two Somua MCG halftrack tractors loaded on railway wagon, Belgium 1943/44

The documents for the following brief development history of the SOMUA half-track vehicles come from Hilary L. Doyle:

MCG 4

Development in the late 1920s, running gear with Kégresse, type P16T track chains. The 4-cylinder carburetor engine had a bore of 82 mm and a stroke of 142 mm and produced 55 hp.

In 1932 it was proposed to use the MCG 4 type as a towing device for the short 155 mm howitzer. A special tractor unit was created for this purpose. It was 4165 mm long and 1888 mm wide. The driver's cab was open at the side and at the front.

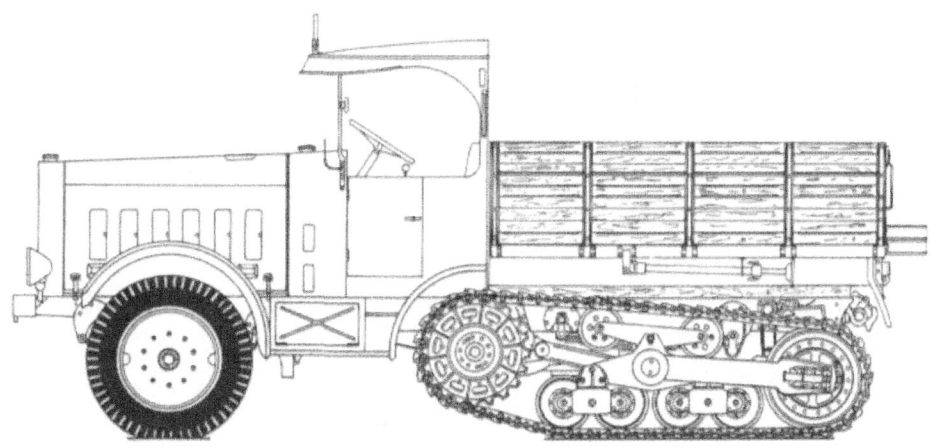

MCG 5

In October 1933 SOMUA presented the successor type MCG 5. The engine power was increased by a new engine, it was now 60hp. The top speed on the road was 40km/h and the driving range was 170km.

Zugkraftwagen Somua MCG S307(f) with PaK 40 in northern italy

The tracks were 300mm wide and an average service life of 8000km was expected. The support roller at the front end of the chassis, fitted to increase the ditch crossing ability, increased the overall length to 5300mm. The MCG weighed 6250kg.

In 1934, SOMUA developed a semi-trailer version of the MCG 5, which was intended to be used as a towing vehicle for the short 155 mm GPF howitzer. The type designation for this version was MCG 11. Early versions had an open driver's cab at the front and side, with later versions the driver's cab was closed. Series production began in 1935, a total of 2543 of these vehicles were built (chassis no. 892-3034), (type MCG 11 3201-3600).

A large number of special superstructures were created for these chassis for the French armed forces, which were then used by the German Wehrmacht after Frances fall in 1940.

MCL 5

Also in October 1933, SOMUA presented the heavier and more powerful version of its half-track vehicles, the MCL 5 type. It was primarily intended as a traction mechanism for the long 155mm GPF gun. The 4-cylinder carburettor engine, type 23, which produced 85hp.

Captured half-track tractor Somua type MCL 5 model 1935

The chain drive was significantly reinforced compared to the MCG 5 type. A semi-trailer version was again selected as the artillery traction mechanism. In 1935, however, the French army decided to have the 155mm guns towed by Laffly S35 wheeled tractors. Nevertheless, a total of about 796 MCL type tractors were built. They were mainly used as recovery vehicles for heavy loads. These vehicles had a reinforced cable winch and a skid that could be lowered at the end of the frame. During its production, the MCL type was continuously further developed.

The Kégresse track was widened to 350mm . Another version was made with steel tracks equipped with a smaller pitch with rubber pads.

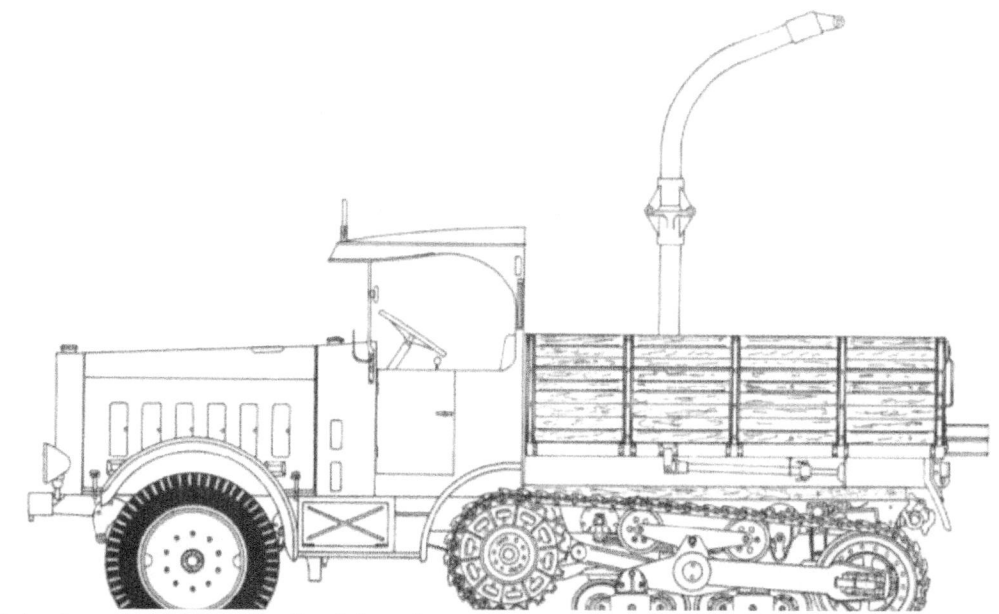

This inevitably resulted in changes to the drive. New drive wheels and idler pulleys as well as two support rollers were typical of these improvements. A third version showed an extended wheelbase to 3090mm. The chain width was now 360mm. In the fourth version, the suspension of the drive was further strengthened.
The final version received widened tracks again. They were now 390mm wide. The new drive wheel received 20 teeth, openings were provided for soil removal. The rollers were supported on an extended suspension.

Weight: 8.50t for the MCL5 and 9.96t for the MCL11

Length: 5.62m for the MCL5 and 5.40m for the MCL11
Width: 2.08m for the MCL5 and 1.95m for the MCL11
Height: 2.33m
Max speed: 31 km/h (4 cylinders, 4712 cm3, 60 hp)

Somua tractor is the type MCL 5 modèle 1935 (source of the pic: "L´automobile sous l´uniforme" by Francois Vauvillier.

The French army used also 148 Somua MCL 5 tractors in tank repair/recovery units.
Weight: 10.9t (live load 2.5t)
Length: 5.48m
Width: 2.10m
Height: 3.00m with crane
Max speed: 31km/h (4 cylinders, 6558cm3, 90hp at 2000rpm)

Captured French Somua MCL half-trackon the Eastern Front towing a Soviet ZIS gun

MSCL 5

An even more powerful tractor was equipped with the 6-cylinder FE engine. It made 105hp. The letter S in the type drawing indicates the 6 cylinder engine. What is remarkable about this engine is the fact that the petrol engine could easily be converted into an 85hp diesel engine. The following chassis number bands were provided for the MCL type: (1732-2099, 2450-2628 and 7002-7250).

Somua towing a Beute cannon, probably with the 32 Infanterie Division

MSCL 12

A proposal by the SOMUA company from 1938 outlines a further reinforcement as a means of towing for the long 155mm gun. A tractor-trailer version was proposed again, this time with 130hp engine. The wheelbase was again increased to 3150mm.

Wehrmacht use of SOMUA Half-tracks
D regulations were issued for the two basic types MCG and MCL, in addition to the usual identification numbers:

- Zugkraftwagen S303 (1), type MCL
- Zugkraftwagen S307 (1), type MCG

Both types were used by Panzerjäger units and artillery units as a means of towing heavy guns (including the 7.5 cm Pak 40). Some were deåloyed with the equipment for the "Schnelle Brigade West" Normandy.

UNIC

The UNIC company provided large numbers of half-track vehicles with various bodies for the French army, navy and air force. About 200 UNIC TU1 U305(f) and 3000 UNIC P107 U304(f) were used by the German army.

UNIC P107 loaded on railcar

Wehrmacht use, note the French numbers are still applied

UNIC P 107BU

The nomenclature of the UNIC P 107 is somewhat complicated by the multiple names that authors have applied to it, such as the "Citroën", " Citroën-Kégresse", "Citroën-Kégresse-Hinston", "UNIC - Kégresse", "Citroën-UNIC ", "UNIC " and others. Since the vast majority of the P 107s that were employed by the French army and, after capture from the French, the German army, were actually manufactured by UNIC , UNIC is the term that I will use. The official German designation for captured UNIC P 107s was the U-304 (f). However, the 21st Panzer Division (the unit which fielded the vast majority of the UNIC s in Normandy) labels them in their Gliederungen as UNIC P 107.

in 1934, the french army launched a call for tenders to replace its aging Citroen P14 artillery semi-tracked tractors. 3,270 machines were delivered to the French Army like many other equipment, part of which was captured by German troops in 1940. (see photo below of a P107 all just leaving the factory).

A factory new UNIC P 107, with WH number plate

Presented on October 4, 1934, the "new Citroën-Kégresse rapid tractor" P 107 is a faster, heavier and considerably more powerful machine than its predecessor, the P 17. wider tread, two notched circles instead of just one on the drive pulley, and a compressed rubber connection between the main balancer and the lower balancers, resulting in very simplified maintenance, elimination of greasing and a smooth, quiet suspension.

The body allows the transport of 6, including the driver, in two 3-seater benches facing the road, 72 rounds of 75 mm transported in 8 boxes (only the boxes need to be changed if the tractor is reassigned), and personnel packs above the ammunition compartment.

Thus presented, the machine received on April 4, 1935 the favorable opinion of the military. After experimentation in the troop corps, the adoption of the P 107 was pronounced, and a contract for 140 copies, including at least 40 artillery type (but also engineer-type flatbeds), was notified to Citroën. August 10, 1935.

In the meantime, André Citroën filed for bankruptcy and died. Behind him, the Michelin brothers, who have taken control of the business, intend to promote mass production and exclude special vehicles. This is how the patent for caterpillar tracks, filed at the end of 1920 under the triple name of Citroën-Kégresse-Hinstin, was transferred at the end of 1935, through the SEK (Kégres operating company), to other manufacturers wishing to continue the light half-track formula: a little at Chenard & Walcker with the latest series of the VLTT P 19, but also and above all at UNIC , specializing in utility vehicles.

Built at the Puteaux factory from the end of 1937, the new tractor received various names, such as Citroën-UNIC , UNIC P 107 B (perhaps indicating the change in engine, the Citroën prototype having first been equipped with a 94 x 110 of 3,060 cm³ developing only 50 hp), P 107 BU or even P 107 U1, the letter U obviously referring to the new manufacturer.

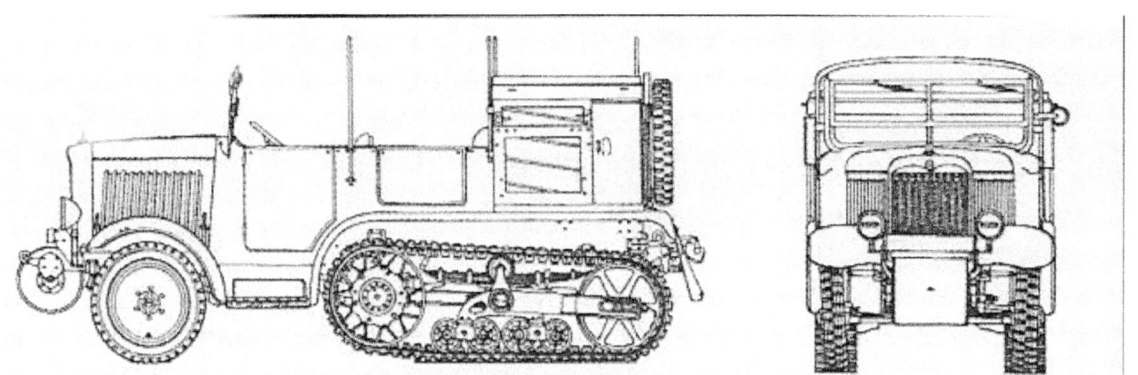

Leichter Artellerie Schlepper UNIC P107 U.304(f)

Here a pic of this tractor out of the book "L'automobile sous l'uniforme" by Francois Vauvillier.

This version was used as a tractor for the 75 mm and 105 mm guns. The superstructure for the ammunition boxes was modified by the Germans

P107 towing artillery

UNIC P107, on a train. a UNIC type P 107BU. This version was used as a tractor for the 75 mm and 105 mm guns. But the superstructure for the ammunition boxes was modified by German coachbuilders

Mittlerer Munitionskraftwagen (munition transporter)

.

The situation in 1939-1940

On September 1, 1939, the light artillery had about 1,450 modern light tractors, Laffly S15 T and Citroën or UNIC P 107. As for the war program, only the latter would be actively produced. "Given the 1,440 old model CK P 17 tractors in service, the rate of delivery of light artillery tractors until March 31, 1940 makes it possible to provide units whose constitution is planned before April 1, 1940, and maintain existing units and have about 525 tractors.
On the other hand, the number of tractors built during the April-September 1940 semester will allow hardly put the mounted artillery units on the TTT type

If the deliveries of tractors are in conformity with the planned deliveries, there will remain about a hundred P 17 tractors in service in the units on September 30, 1940 ." (SAET, December 23, 1939).

The Laffly S15 T and UNIC P 107 tractors are indiscriminately assigned to the groups of 75mm guns on tires (the most frequent case) but also to the new 105mm short light artillery equipment.

On May 15, 1940, "< the shortage of our manpower in horses will oblige to form the majority of the new units of artillery on the auto type". The program then aims, as for light artillery, to put on tires".

There are then 53 groups of 75 TTT and 13 towed groups of 105C, as well as 7 TTT batteries of 75mm anti-tank (6 pieces). On December 1, 1939, the GOG lists 2,624 light tractors mobilized in the armies plus 52 in the formations of the territory.

On September 3, 1939, the French army had 1,066 P 107 artillery tractors, producing in peacetime at around 120 ex./month. On August 27, Poland ordered 60 copies. which, exceptional case, are delivered or almost: on September 22, 40 of them, including 29 embarked in Brest and the others already at sea, are recalled and reassigned to the French army. Given the promptness of UNIC's reaction to the Polish order, these vehicles had, one suspects, been taken from the manufacturing chain.

The mobilization order, modified on September 11, 1939, relates to 900 P 107 artillery tractors including 730 for the traction of the 75mm in mainland France and 170 AFN type, quantities to which will be added 1,570 ex. for 75mm guns ordered on September 17.

A UNIC P107 towing a leFH 18 on dolly trailer, rather unique picture

A UNIC P107 towing a leFH 18 on dolly trailer, rather unique picture

Slovakia 1944, German captured UNIC P107- Zugkraftwagen U304(f)

A P107 semi track loaded onto a railway wagon

UNIC P107 towing a Germna Wehrmacht 4 wheel Sd. Anh

This photo was probably taken in Wieliczka, in Poland. Teodor Sapiński was vicemayor of Wieliczka in 1922-1930, and his family had a house and grocery at Rynek Górny 10 address

Almost unique in the history of the manufacture of special vehicles in 1939-1940, the production rate set at 250 ex./month from February 1940 was not only respected by UNIC , but exceeded (table p. 161). The total built will have reached 3,276 ex. (all military and civilian types) of P 107 when production stopped at Puteaux in early June 1940.

Number of cylinders:4
Max Power: 62 hp at 2,800 rpm
Number of gears: 2x (4+ reverse)
Displacement: 3,460 cc
Wheelbase: 2,55 m
Front track: 1,40 m
Rear track: 1,34 m
Length: 4,85 m
Width: 1,80 m
Weight:3500kg
Payload: 1 500 kg
Towed load: 1,500 kg
Height : 2,30 m
Max. Speed: 45 km/h

Leichter Artillerieschlepper P107 U304(f)

UNIC P107 half-track and PaK 38

A collection of Zugkraftwagen

Halftrack UNIC with 5cm PaK 38

Captured French UNIC P 107 tractor of a 150 mm infantry gun (sIG 33) in Russia

SS unit in Soviet union August 1941

SS numberplate here differs only one digit from the above,

UNIC P107 with trailer, Operation Barbarossa, Soviet Union, August 1941. Same unit as the pictures above

French 25mm Anti tank gun, with UNIC P107

Motor repair of a UNIC P107

Good picture of the UNIC tracks, and the unmodified cab

UNIC used to tow PaK 36

UNIC TU 1

TU1 was an french abbreviation for Tracteur d'infanterie UNIC TU 1, or tractor for the infantry.

The TU1 was adopted in September 1939 as an infantry tractor for the 25mm anti-tank gun. The first deliveries began in April 1940, much too late to equip the existing divisions. The 236 units available served as a supply tractor in the new anti-tank batteries equipped with the LAFFLY W15TCC.

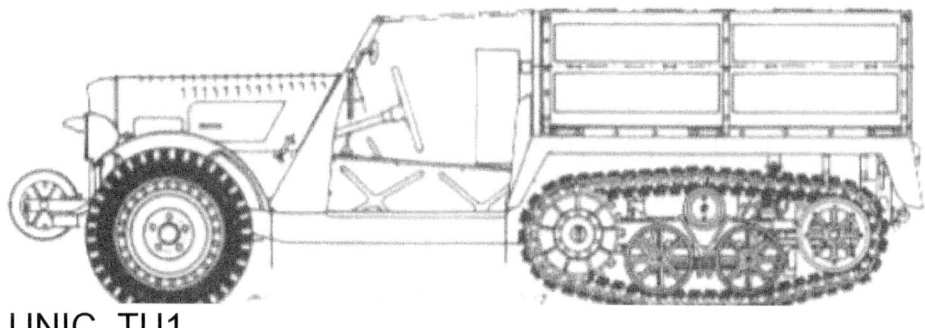

UNIC TU1

After the fall of france, production continued for the benefit of the Germans, who adopted it under the name of Zugkraftwagen UNIC TU1 U305(f). The machine was used as a light artillery tractor (Leichter Artillrieschlepper) but also as a recovery vehicle (Bergefahrzeug) or as a training vehicle (Fahrschulfahrzeug)

Engine: UNIC   M16D ohv, 2200cc, 4 cylinders with liquid cooling, maximum power: 50 hp
Weight: 2,500 kg
Payload: 500 kg
Length: 4.2 m
Width: 1.52 m
Height: 1.31 m
Max speed. : 46 km/h

This intelligent vehicle is at the confluence of the two categories of light tractors since it is presented in January 1939, both for the traction of the 25 mm cannon and for that of the infantry cart model 1937. Its essential characteristic is to see driving for a long time at the speed of columns on foot (4 km/h in first gear with a reduction gear) as well as that of car convoys, despite a somewhat low maximum speed (46 km/h instead of 60), not affecting hardly the average of 35 km/h.

Its half track a new design, the entire running gear (rollers, sprocket and tension pulley being fixed on a spar oscillating freely from top to bottom; the caterpillar is metal with steel pads fitted with rubber. This thruster suffered from a few clearance defects and, on May 26, 1939, after improvement, the TU 1 prototype was again presented and accepted.

UNIC TU-1/Zugkraftwagen U-305 (f)

The TU1 covered tractor, highlights the exceptionally low relief of this vehicle intended to weave its way with the infantry under cover.

Zugkraftwagen UNIC TU1 U305(f), with trailer

On September 12, 1939, 1000 ex. were ordered, increased to 1120 on December 23, with delivery no later than September 30, 1940. The first 10 TU 1s were delivered during the week of March 31 to April 5. These few weeks of delay on the forecasts prevented a large entry into service of the TU 1. The light half-track which was initially intended for the transport of heavy armament of motorized infantry units, and more particularly for traction of the new 20 mm CA 39 Oerlikon machine gun (12 per motorized infantry regiment), will be used, given the urgency, for other jobs, in particular as a supply tractor within the batteries of tank destroyers Laffly W15 TCC (2 UNIC TU 1, towing a 1937 model cart, 200 strokes per team).

Below, the same vehicle, tarpaulins and canvas doors rolled up. Good accessibility to the front seats and rear cargo

Payload was 500 kg and a trailer with 660kg

Zgkw U 305 (1), type TU 1. First vehicle delivered on March 28, 1940, by June 1940 a total of 236 units, almost all of which were taken over by the German Wehrmacht (chassis no. 106 001-106236).

By the Wehrmacht it was used as follows:
- Message motor vehicle The light towing vehicle TU 1 (identification number U305(1) was used as
- light artillery tractor
- Rescue vehicle (makeshift) used. The 4th Panzer Division, 35th Panzer Regiment, used some TU 1s as driving school vehicles during training.

The overall assessment of the troop was negative: the UNIC TU1 tractors did not prove their worth, as the running gear, engine and electrical system were constantly being damaged.

Fall of France

After the end of the French campaign, captured British, French, Dutch and Belgian vehicles were collected and gathered together in depots. Due to the heavy vehicle casualties suffered by the German units that participated in the Western Campaign and the insufficient availability of German-produced replacement vehicles, many French and British and, to a lesser degree, Dutch and Belgian vehicles were used to refit these units. Also, at this time, new divisions were being created and some of these were almost completely equipped with French vehicles. According to Spielberger, "in 1941 alone, 88 German infantry divisions, 3 infantry divisions (Motorized) and one panzer division could be equipped in their entirety with French motor vehicles" (Beute, Pg. 51). Nonetheless, large stocks of vehicles remained unused in depots in France up to late 1942.

Baukommando Becker was established in Maison-Lafitte in northern Paris to exploit the existing stocks of captured vehicles with the aim of rehabilitating and converting them for the use by the Wehrmacht. This will be discussed in more detail later on.

The main sources of information for this piece are Vauvillier's book on the armored vehicles of the French Army up to 1940 and Spielberger's book on captured vehicles of the Wehrmacht. Spielberger lists the Becker Archives as one of his sources; however, the photographs are not individually attributed but rather the total numbers of photographs used in the book are listed per source. According to this information, 162 photos(in Spielbergers book) are from Alfred Becker's collection, most of which show the vehicles in "portraits" after they had already been delivered to and integrated by Schnelle Brigade West or by its precursor units. In addition, photos were taken within the factories themselves showing various vehicles being overhauled, photos of scrap yards showing piles of parts and vehicle carcasses as well as *Aufbaus* being fabricated for other vehicles. There are not, however, many photos of beute vehicles being used in the field. Many of the photos used in this piece are taken from this book.

Baukommando Becker

Major Alfred Becker was put in charge of repurpose of French equipment left in France after the fall of France. This was after he had proven it was viable on the Eastern front, the goal from the Ober Kommando der Wehrmacht(OKW) was to rebuilt the 21st Panzer division in 1943, but the 21st were not to request any new vehicles from German factories as they were under heavy attack by allied bombers and production went to other fronts. Becker was chosen because he and his soldiers had done the same in 1940-41 with material from the defeat of the British and Belgian Army. These vehicles had been successfully used on the Eastern front. The main idea at the time by Becker was to mechanize his horsedrawn artillery battery, a 10.5cm Howitzer battery witn ammonution carriers and spotting vehicles.

The idea was of cause to be ready to fire the battery quicker than by a horse drawn unit, the next thing was that the crew of a single 10.5cm howitzer went down from a crew of 6 to 4 men

To this he used rebuilt British Mark IV tanks(e), both as self propelled guns (SPG), but also as Beobachtungspanzer) observation tanks, with radio equipment) and bren gun carriers used as ammunition transports.

The task before Becker was enormous. There was a huge quantity of allied military vehicles throughout France in various states and conditions. A number of the French armoured vehicles that were undamaged had already been in use, either as training vehicles or sent abroad to equip various units, usually to an Axis allied nation or a police unit, but these vehicles were often limited by a small, one man turret that mounted an underpowered gun. They were unsuitable for combat against such weapons as the Russian KV-1, KV-2 and T-34. As to the wrecks and other vehicles left behind, though a large number of these French tanks in various states of condition still remained, these vehicles were of limited usefulness for combat in 1942. Up to this point, their primary use to the German army was as a symbol of their victory against France. Though these were lightly armoured and undergunned by combat standards of the day, they were fully tracked vehicles that Becker believed could be usefully exploited. In addition to the abandoned and wrecked French and British tanks, Becker had access to a large number of soft-skinned French half-tracked vehicles such as the SOMUA MCG and the smaller UNIC P 107.

Wooden mock-up of Schutzen Panzer Wagen(SPW) by Becker on an UNIC chassis

Setting up headquarters at Maisons-Laffitte, the vehicles were collected at the Hotchkiss works near Paris, where Becker established his Baukommando Becker (Construction Unit Becker). Becker's basic idea for the conversion was straightforward in principle: Becker produced a prototype of the new superstructure out of wood, which was sent to Alkett. Alkett then produced the steel superstructures for the run. These were then sent back to France, where Becker had completed the engineering plans for the conversion. Alkett was a subsidiary of Rheinmetall-Borsig AG and was short for Altmärkische Kettenweke(Altmark Trackfactory).

Picture of another Alfred Becker prototype, by the Becker Baukommando, Paris

The Hotchkiss assembly line was then brought up again, the conversion process was streamlined and a run of assembly was completed. The vehicles where repaired by importance, all of one type in one step. All remaining spare parts were stored away. Any remaining material was shipped back to the steelworks.

The innovative aspect of the work was the battle value assessment of the vehicles, determining the most effective future use of each vehicle type as part of the German war effort in relation to the existing demands. This was then coupled with an accurate classification of each model. The vehicles were divided into three groups: those requiring minor repairs and refits, those requiring major repair and refits, and those that were beyond use and were to be used as a source for spare parts. Becker was assigned an engineering staff, who set about their work of modifying what was available, and soon they were producing a variety of innovative designs. Among those vehicles being used was a considerable number of Lorraine tractors, about 360 of which had fallen into German hands. Due to its reliability, the Lorraine was well suited to the maneuvre warfare battles the Germans favoured. They were first used as tractors to pull German artillery pieces, and were renamed the Lorraine Schlepper (f). As the Germans themselves had not produced a similar vehicle, the Lorraine tractors filled a requirement for fully tracked artillery and supply vehicles, badly needed due to the extremely poor road conditions in Russia.

From 1942 through 1943 Becker salvaged all usable tank wreckage he found in France, creating some 1,800 armoured fighting vehicles. From July to August, 1942, Becker converted 170 armoured vehicles into the Marder I, a 75 mm self-propelled anti-tank gun, plus a further 106 chassis were converted into self-propelled artillery pieces, with 94 conversions to carry the 150 mm howitzer, and 12 more to carry the 105 mm. In addition, he produced 30 artillery observation vehicles, using this same chassis.

Schnelle Brigade West had 60 of these UNIC P 107

During this time, Becker's old unit, the 227th Infantry Division, was engaged in heavy fighting near Leningrad during the Red Army's main offensive at Sinyavino Heights and the south shore of Lake Ladoga. From August through September 1942 the division suffered heavy casualties in what was called the Battle of Lake Ladoga. Becker was concerned for his men in the 15th Artillery Regiment. For the conversion work Becker was attempting, these men understood the theory and practice of the conversions, and had combat experience of the weapons in action as well. Becker considered them ideal to his purposes. He requested the transfer of his surviving men from the 15th Artillery back to his command in Paris, and this took place at Christmas 1942. As part of the agreement, Baustab Becker provided the 227th Infantry Division with some 20 armored artillery vehicles.

Refurbishment of UNIC P107 in Paris

In 1943 Becker began converting the Hotchkiss H35 and H39 light tanks, which had carried a 37 mm gun, and refit them to mount a 7.5 cm PaK40 anti-tank gun or 10.5 cm leFH16 howitzer assault gun. These were the units that were used extensively in the equipping of the reformed 21st Panzer Division, and can be seen in images of Rommel reviewing the unit in May 1944.

Refurbishment of UNIC P107 in Paris

Another major project Becker undertook was the work he did on the soft-skinned French half-tracked vehicles, the SOMUA MCG and the smaller UNIC P 107. Both of these vehicles he armoured to make them more survivable in the battle environment. The SOMUA MCG he used as a platform for a number of weapons, including the Vielfachwerfer, and the Reihenwerfer, his own creation of more than a battery of up to twenty 81 mm mortars. The smaller UNIC P107 light halftrack was also armoured and used primarily as a self propelled weapon (SPW) as a substitute for the Sd.Kfz. 251, which was prohibited to the Schnelle Brigade West(they where urgently needed on the Eastern Front).

On March 15, 1943 Major Becker's unit, the gepanzerte Artillerie Brigade of Schnelle Brigade West, participated in a memorial to the men of 15 Batterie Artillerie Regiment 227, killed in action during the Leningrad siege of 1941-42. Becker and his officers laid wreaths in their memory. A memory to his soldiers that died before he could get them transferred to the Baukommando. Skilled Krefeld welders and metalworkers.

In the spring of 1943 Albert Speer and his entourage paid a visit to General Feuchtinger, Major Becker, and the Matford factory which was one of the facilities involved in the conversion work. Film taken at this time show the visitors examining a French FCM tank and a French Somua halftrack, both converted to carry the 7.5 cm PaK 40 anti-tank gun. They also examined a Somua halftrack fitted with the Reihenwerfer, a rack of 2x8(16) French 81.4 mm Brandt mortars and a Renault UE Beobachtungspanzer. Over the course of 1943 a number of other high ranking German officers visited Baukommando Becker, including Gerd von Rundstedt, and in August 1943, Heinz Guderian.

For this book we will only look at the Half tracks constructed, but the work of the Baukommando was very extensive. They where involved in making cars, motorcycles, Tanks, tank destroyers, self propelled artillery and in general overhauling former french vehicles. The Germans at the time in 1943 had already trouble with manufacturing, so it was decided on that the Schnelle Brigade west, could not get any German produced material due the need for material on the Eastern front. This was the preparation for the operation Zitadelle(Battle of Kursk). The preparation was stalled again and again not only due to problems with the Panzer kampfwagen V Panther, but also other pet projekts of Adolf Hitler.

On a side note here i will note that the battle of Kursk of cause was a German loss, but in the process of that they chewed up a newly formed elite Soviet Guards division, and that alone prolonged the war with nearly a year. Thats how effective the new 7.5cm KwK was.

Brandt mortars being fitted to Vielwerfer chassis

Zugkraftwagen Somua MCG S307(f)

The SOMUA MCG was a half-track artillery tractor and recovery vehicle of the French forces during World War II.

Manufactured by the Somua company it was used to tow medium artillery pieces such as the 155 mm mle 1917 howitzer and the 105 mm mle 1936 field gun, as well as their specific ammunition trailers. Of this main version 345 were produced: 264 until 1 September 1939 and another 81 until the end of May 1940.

After France's surrender, many Somua MCG and MCL half-tracks were captured by the Germans and put to use in the German army. Some were used as artillery tractors. Some were converted by Major Alfred Becker's workshop (Baukommando Becker) into armoured half-tracks. Variants of these included an armoured rocket launcher

with an 8 cm Raketen-Vielfachwerfer, a self-propelled mortar mounting an 8 cm Reihenwerfer multiple mortar array and a tank destroyer version with a 75 mm Pak 40 anti-tank gun.
There was also a recovery version, fitted with a crane, to recover broken-down tanks, of these about 440 were produced.

Weight: 6.8 t
Length: 5.30 m
Width: 2.17 m
Height: 2.85 m
Crew: 2 + 8 passengers
Engine: 4-cylinder, petrol, 4712 cc 60 hp
Payload capacity: 1500 kg
Maximum speed: 31 km/h

Munitions-Zugkraftwagen Somua MCG S307(f) (48 produced)

A Munitionskraftwagen auf Somua MCG 5-Fahrgestell during the Battle of the Bulge

48 of these armoured ammumitions transports was delievered by Becker, from SOMUA MCG

In 1943, some Somua MCG S307(f) were converted to mittlere schutzen panzerwagen(mSPW) S307(f), equivalent of the Sdkfz 251/1

In 1943, some Somua MCG S307(f) were converted to pioneer Panzerwagen mSPW S307(f), equivalent of the Sdkfz 251/7

In 1943, 72 Somua MCG S307 (f) were converted to 7,5cm Pak40 (Sf) auf mSPW S307(f), equivalent of the Sdkfz 251/22 (72 produced).

8cm Leichter Reihenwerfer auf SPW Somua S307(f), 16x 81mm Brandt mortars on a single mount (36 produced)

Leichter Reihenwerfer auf SOMUA MCG

Both SOMUA types played an important role in the Baukommando Becker construction detail. The majority of these vehicles were armored, although it must be mentioned that the scarcity of materials in those years made adequate armor impossible, since the quality of the armor plates and their processing left a lot to be desired. Almost all vehicles converted by Major Alfred Becker were based on the MCG chassis,

Light row launcher with 16 barrels In the rear part of the vehicle, 16 grenade launcher barrels (today mortar barrels) were arranged in two rows on a 360° rotatable platform. The launcher grenades were held in place by a holding device attached to the upper end of the tube and were fired either individually or in salvos. The official designation was »RG 16 row thrower shooting device. The elevation of the barrel was 40 to 90 degrees

Panzerjäger with 7.5-cm-Pak 40.

7.5cm PaK 40 auf Somua S307(f), (PaK - Panzer abwehr Kanone, Anti-tank gun)

Not a great photo quality, bur a PaK 40 auf Somua somewhere in Normandy

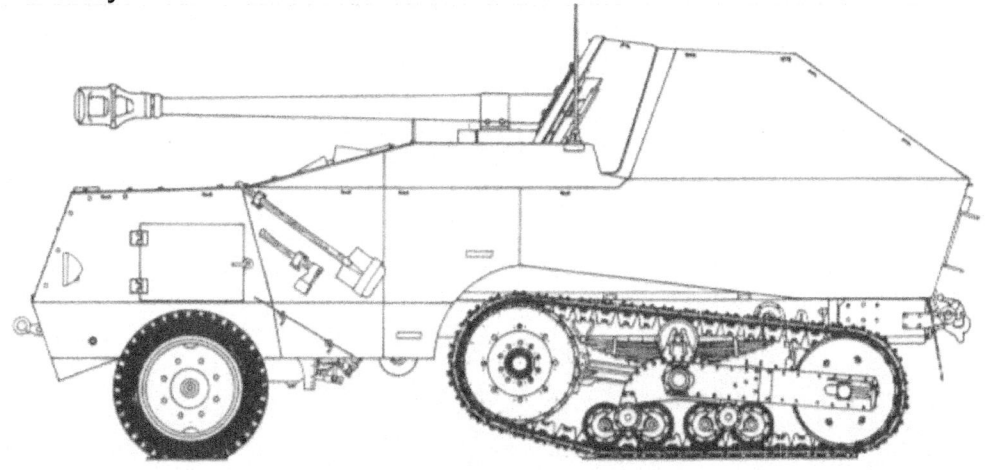

Drawing, sideways view of the Somua Panzerjaeger

A new Somua Panzerjaeger in Paris, right out of Baukommando Becker Factory

A well comuflaged Panzerjaeger during training

Training in Normandy in May with the Somua Panzerjaeger, here showing in a prepared dug out position, to gain a lower profie

The construction of these Somua panzerjaeger apparently predates the construction of the Sd. Kfz 251/22

By 1943, 72 Somua MCG S307 (f) were converted to 7,5cm Pak40 (Sf) auf mSPW S307(f), equivalent of the Sdkfz 251/22. Knocked out in Normandy

Pioneer Panzerwagen mSPW S307(f), equivalent of the Sdkfz 251/7

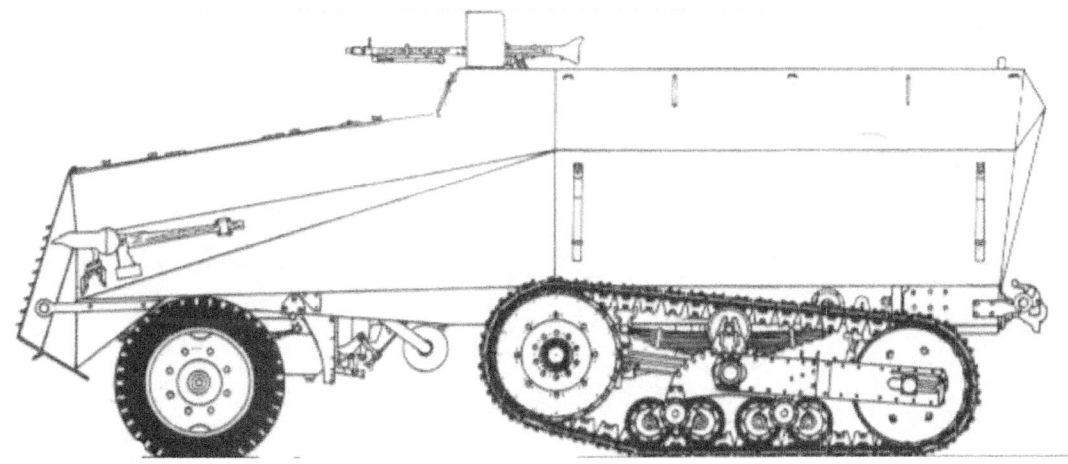

Pioneer variant, note the sleek body

Note here on the SOMUA Pioneer variant, the trench crossing equipment is not mounted over the tracks

In 1943, Somua MCG S307(f) were converted to pioneer Panzerwagen mSPW S307(f), equivalent of the Sdkfz 251/7. Note bridging equipment mounted over the tracks, Pioneer variant

Reihenwerfers

This weapon system was the only one of its kind and developed at the Baukommando. The combination or bondling of 16-20 mortars into one platform firing a salvo like that. Normally each Grenadier or infantry company had a heavy weapons platoon, and it had assigned a 8cm mortar.

These Brandt Mle 27/31mortars had a range of between 1.2km to 2.8km. Original it was a development of the Stokes mortar. Pre WW2 the mortar was widely used in European armies. Uses included Austria,Denmark, Norway, France, Netherlands, Poland and Yugoslavia just to name the countries conquored by Germany.

There seems to be some confusion about the Reihenwerfers in other publications. Spielberger obtained his info directly from Becker as he cites the "Alfred Becker private archive" as one of his sources and states that there were 36 light Reihenwerfers (MCG) and 16 heavy

Reihenwerfers (MCL) created by Baustab Becker). Kortenhaus states that the 10.Kompanie of both Pz.-Gren.Rgt. 125 & 192 were equipped with "vier Reihenwerfer, je 24 Rohren 8,14 cm" (four Reihenwerfers, each with 24 8.14 cm mortar tubes). Neither of the types of Reihenwerfer made by Becker as per his archives had 24 tubes. However Spielberger states the allocation as: "10.Werfer-Kompanie mit vier Reihenwerfer 8,14 cm (16 Rohre) auf SOMUA MCG (f)" where "16 Rohre" is the 16 mortar tubes, the correct number for the light Reihenwerfer.

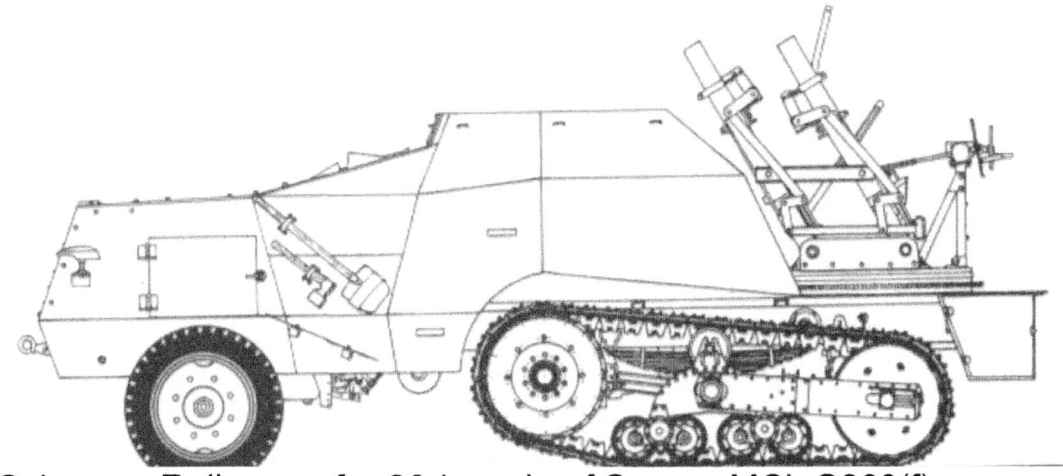

Schwerer Reihenwerfer 20-barrel auf Somua MCL S303(f)

Light row launcher with 16 barrels In the rear part of the vehicle, 16 grenade launcher barrels (today mortar barrels) were arranged in two rows on a 360° rotatable platform. The launcher grenades were held in place by a holding device attached to the upper end of the tube and were fired either individually or in salvos. The official designation was »RG 16 row thrower shooting device. The elevation of the barrel was 40 to 90 degrees.

Schwerer Vielfachwerfer 20-barrels

Schwerer Reihenwerfer auf SOMUA MCL

Because of the armor, the fully and partially armored carrier vehicles were given a modified cooler and fan system compared to the original vehicles, which was lower in construction and thus reduced the target it represented.

The MCL chassis was used for:
- 20-barrel heavy in-line launcher, also using French 8.14cm D 278 (f) grenade launchers.(16 produced)
They where used by the heavy companies. The device was first presented in 1943 in Hillersleben.
- Rocket launcher with 48 shots (6 pieces) The 8cm rocket launcher was a mobile launching ramp for 48 rockets in two layers one above the other. 12 guide rails each. Lateral adjustment range 360 degrees by handwheel operation. Launcher elevation was 45 degrees. The programmed firing sequence allowed the firing of all rockets in one salvo of all 48 missiles.

8cm Raketten-Vielfachwerfer auf Somua S303 (f)

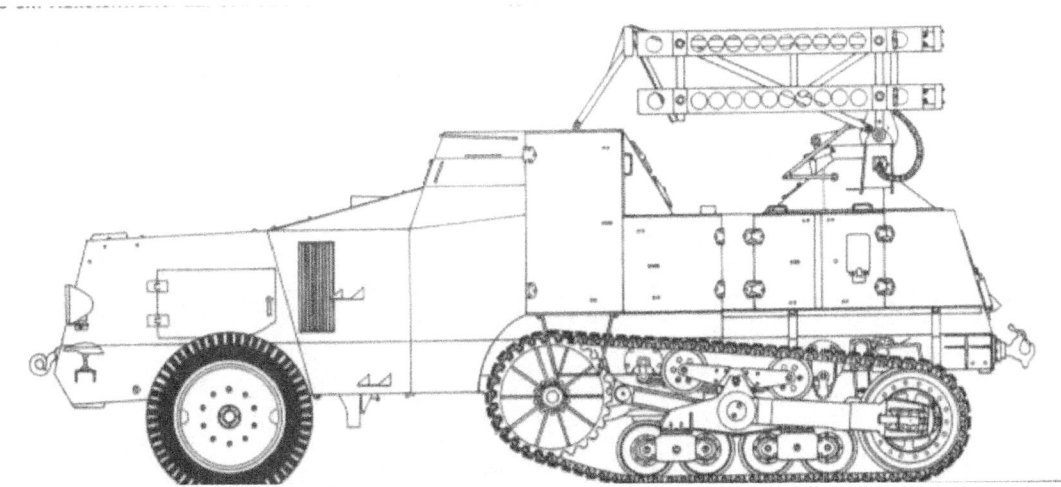

For Ammunition they had wing-stabilized rockets, caliber 8 cm. Smoke and explosive projectiles (these rockets could also be fired from aircraft).
Hitler ordered a large-scale testing of this weapon system in March 1944. It was to be used primarily by Waffen-SS units.
Weight of the launcher (with two loads of ammunition) 6850kg Weight of the launcher 6200kg(without ammunition) The length of the

launcher was 1860mm, the maximum range of the weapon was 5300m.

The vehicle carried:
- Explosive shells 232 rounds
- Smoke shells 56 rounds

8cm Raketten-Vielfachwerfer auf Somua S303 (f), mounting 2 racks of 80mm rockets – the vehicle carried 232 HE and 56 smoke rockets (6 produced)

These Rakettenwerfers are sometimes incorrectly referred to as UNIC P 107's, but they are based on the SOMUA MCL.

After the war, one of these armored half-tracks was equipped by the French army with a 15 cm Panzerwerfer 42 (10x) of German design. It stayed with this attempt.

Leichte Zugkraftwagen P 107 (Kenn-Nummer U304(f))

Most of the vehicles that fell into German hands undamaged were assigned to German units. It was up to the Becker Baukommando to repair the remains, no matter how badly damaged, and to equip them with other superstructures, some of them armored, which were used almost exclusively by the Schnelle Brigade West.

The light tractor UNIC P107 (identification number U304(1) appeared as:

- medium ammunition truck
- light artillery tractor
- light personnel carrier (unarmored) with machine gun trailer (60 units at Brigade West)")
- recovery vehicles (makeshift)
- light armored personnel carrier**) (closed and open body), platoon driver's car with 3.7 cm Pak 36
- Self-propelled gun (partially armored) for 2 cm Flak 38
- Self-propelled gun (armored) for 2 cm Flak 38 (72 units in Brigade West). 360° side alignment field.
- Grenade launcher tank
- Medical tank
- Funkkraftwagen (armoured)

The 1st Battalion of the Panzergrenadier Regiment was armored, the 2nd Battalion remained unarmoured. Despite all emergency measures, the height of the armored vehicles was only 20 cm more than the bodies of German manufacture (Sd.Kfz. 251). Two groups with either 2 machine guns or one machine gun and a heavy grenade launcher (mortar) were loaded onto the personnel carrier.

The UNIC P107 that was refurbished by Baukommando Becker was used in various different roles. The vehicles created in the Hotchkiss works in Paris was all to be used for reconstruction of the 21st Panzer Division, this was at first know as the Schnelle Brigade West(Fast brigade west).

All armies, whether it be due to necessity, curiosity, preference or mere opportunity, use weapons and equipment that are captured from the enemy. Arguably no other army in modern times, however, has utilized captured foreign ordnance to such an extent as the Wehrmacht during World War II. A central figure in this utilization, as far as Western beute materials goes, was Hauptmann (later Major) Alfred Becker.

At the start of the Blitzkrieg, Becker was the commander of the 12. Batterie (or 15. Batterie, the sources conflict) of the artillery battalion of the 227. Infanterie-Division - a horse-drawn unit. In Amersfoort, Holland, Becker gathered up captured Dutch and Belgian trucks, cars and motorcycles to fully motorize his "officially" horse-drawn battery. After the capitulation of France, Becker, apparently, again, on his own initiative, gathered up some abandoned British Vickers Mk. VI light tanks and by removing the turret and part of the upper structure and adding to it an armored body and 10.5cm Field Howitzer 16s (leFH16) was able to construct a full battery of 6 vehicles (Spielberger, Jentz). These guns were taken by the 227. Infanterie-Division to Russia where they performed favorably according to surviving reports and Becker's Self Propelled(SP) Batterie made a name for itself.

In August 1942, OKH requested that one of Becker's SP guns be sent to Berlin and on Sept 2 Becker and a crew demonstrated it before Hitler in the garden of the Reichs Chancellory. This iImpressed Hitler and he later sent Becker to Alkett as a consultant and for then to Paris to oversee the renovation, rebuilding and conversion of the stocks of captured vehicles stored there, as well as collecting parts from battlefield wrecks and scrap yards.

The patterns for the aufbaus for converted vehicles were created by Alkett and Becker and sent to selected French factories for assembly-line production. Spare parts were cannibalized from wrecks and stripped clean and/or rebuilt resulting in practically new vehicles and also a supply of spare parts. The BaukommandoBecker restored or converted approximately 1800 vehicles, the vast majority of which were used to equip the Schnelle Brigade West, which was created in 1943. This number comes from Spielberger's book but it is unclear if this is a final or an intermediate number.

On 2 July 1944, Major Becker of the 21. Armored Division, who at that time was commander of the Sturmgeschütz-Abteilung 200, was recommended for the award of the *Ritterkreuzes zum*

Kriegsdienstkreuz mit Schwerter or the Knight's Cross of the War Service Cross with Swords. This medal was awarded at the end of 1944.

The UNIC P 107

The UNIC P 107 was primarily produced for the French Army and as such the majority were used as artillery tractors.

In addition to the artillery version for the the French army, there was also an Engineer version,

a version for the Air Force and also a version for use in North Africa and two were also some fitted as signals vehicles.

The French Army impressed some that had been produced for civilian use after war broke out in 1939. According to Vauvillier (Pg. 199), a total of 3276 P 107s - including all military and civilian versions - and these were produced by the beginning of June 1940 at which time production ceased. Spielberger backs this figured up.

The total number of UNIC P 107s impressed into German service as well as the numbers of the various subtypes is very difficult to determine. While Spielberger includes a few lists of numbers of vehicles, the vehicle types are often ambiguously indicated by purpose instead of make and some of the numbers do not make much sense. Being German, production records were certainly meticulously maintained and reported to at least one but probably more than one higher authority, perhaps the Reichsministeriums für Rüstung und Kriegsproduktion and the Waffenamt. I have not been able to locate these records yet, if they survived the war.

Unfortunately, any non-armored P 107s are not mentioned in most sources, but it is quite possible that there were a large number serving in many of the subunits of 21st Panzer as well as other units in Normandy.

While the majority of P 107s that were refurbished and/or modified by

Baukommando Becker were allocated to Schnelle Brigade West, which later became the 21st Panzer Division, it is possible that others were issued to other divisions. It appears that all of the armored P 107s were issued to 21st Panzer Division but there is ample photographic evidence that unarmored P 107s were used by other units, especially during the early years in the Balkans and on the Eastern Front.

The UNIC s that were issued to German units before Baukommando Becker was established were for the most part minimally converted. The most common modification was the addition of covers to the headlights.

The UNIC P 107 was converted by the Germans to play numerous roles. While some were extensively converted with armored bodies and/or the addition of weapons, the majority was just thoroughly overhauled.

The UNIC s that have been documented - the armored ones - were located in five subunits of the 21st Panzer Division:
Pz.-Gren.-Rgt. 125
Pz.-Gren.-Rgt. 192
Sturmgeschütz Abt. 200
Pz. Nachrichten Abt. 200
Pz.-Pio.-Batt. 200.
In addition, the 1st and 3rd Companies of the Feldersatz Batt. 200 were armored, thus it is probable that these companies were equipped also with UNICs. These were probably unarmored UNICs, though it is almost certain that these also made up part of the complement of 21. Panzer Division's motorized vehicles. These were probably reported together with other softskin trucks as a *Lastkraftwagen* in the various reports.

Unarmored UNIC s

Medium ammunition carrier
- mittlerer Munitionskraftwagen

Light artillery tractors
- leichter Artillerieschlepper

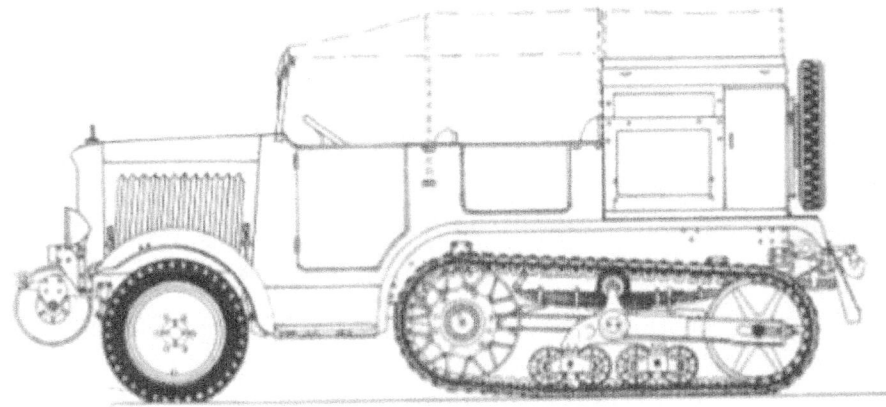

Leichter Zugkraftwagen UNIC P107, Artellerie Schlepper ausfuhrung

Light unarmored personnel carriers with MG trailer

- leichter Mannschaftstransportwagen (ungepanzert) mit MG-Anhänger (60 Stück bei der Brigade West)")

Schnelle Brigade West had 60 of these UNIC P 107

This example of a *Mannschafttransportwagen* (ungepanzert) is of a P 107 with benches added to the rear to act as a non-armored personnel carrier. 60 examples was used by the Schnelle Brigade West:

Provisional recovery vehicles
- Bergefahrzeuge (behelfsmäßig)

There were apparently a number of P 107s set aside for towing lighter vehicles. Due to the P 107's relatively low towing power (and the designation "provisional"), their employment in this role was probably a result of the insufficient availability of proper vehicles for this role. It is unknown if any P 107s were used by 21st Panzer in this function. This example is in use by an NSKK unit. Date and location unknown:

Signals vehicle
- Nachrichtenkraftwagen

No known photos. It is unknown how many were adapted for this role and how many were maintained, if any, by 21st Panzer Division.

Light unarmored tractors, engineer variant

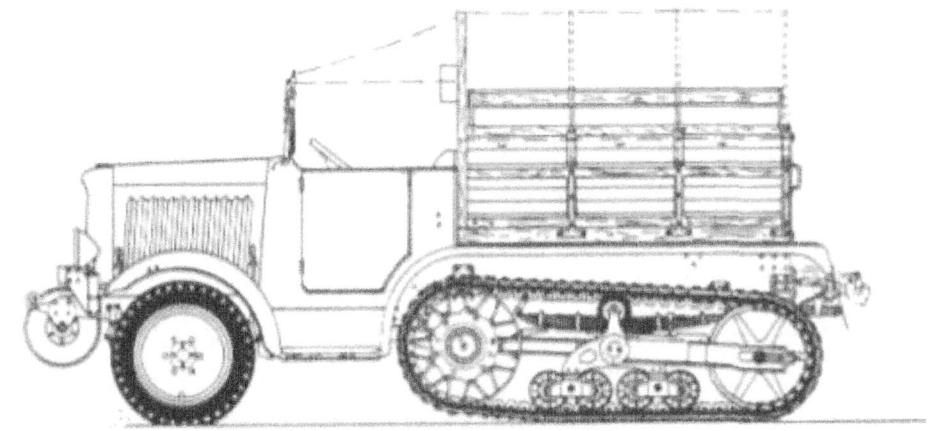

Leichter Zugkraftwagen UNIC P107, Pioneer Schlepper ausfuhrung

Armored UNIC

Leichter Artillerieschlepper P107 U304(f) (to tow 3.7cm Pak36, 7.5cm Pak97/38, 7.5cm PaK40, 10.5cm leFH18). Note Wehrmacht number plate, factory new. Leichter Mannschaftstransportwagen (with a wooden open-top compartment to transport troops)

Light armored personnel carriers Aufbau offen
  - leichter Schützenpanzerwagen (Aufbau geschlossen und offen),

There were two versions of armored bodies (or aufbaus) produced by the Germans for the UNIC (other than the Flakpanzer version). The first version (Aufbau offen) had a body that consisted of sides composed of two plates with the bottom-most plate being set more or less at a 90° angle and the top, smaller plate being slightly angled inward towards the interior of the crew compartment. It appears that Aufbau offen UNIC was used only in the armored personnel carrier role. While I have not seen any photographs with MG34 or MG42 mounted on any Aufbau offen UNIC s, there is a photo of a prototype which has an MG42 attached to the passenger side front of the armored cab.

Armoured UNIC P107 ausf 1 Kenn nummer U304(f), crew and troops dismounted

There are a fairly large number of photos of UNIC s taken on the battlefields of Normandy. A few of these were taken shortly before D-Day by the members of the unit to which they belonged, but most were taken by British, Canadian or American official photographers and others taken by regular soldiers and civilians. Most of these with some exceptions are difficult if not impossible to date and locate.

SPW Aufbau offen, With driver and commander and 8 troops

Light armored personnel carriers Aufbau geschlossen

The Aufbau geschlossen body type was probably the more common body and was used for all of the armored variations, with the exception of the 2 cm flak versions. The body of the Aufbau geschlossen. has more complex angles, similar to those of the Sd.Kfz. 251 Ausf. A, B & C.

The Armored SPW UNIC P107 seems very high but in fact only 20cm higher than a SdKfz-251/1 (SPW - Schützen Panzer Wagen, Infantry Armoured car).

Most were opened topped, but a few command and/or signals versions were constructed with a roof.

The majority of the Aufbau geschlossen UNIC s were employed in the role of armored personnel carriers. These normally were equipped with pintles for MG 42 at the front and rear of the fighting compartment. According to Kortenhaus (App., Pg. 585) the 4th Platoon of each Panzer Grenadier Company of the I. Battalion of both Regiments was the heavy platoon and was equipped with 4 SPW with heavy MGs, so, one would assume, these were equipped with the s.MG Lafette or a Heavy.MG tripod

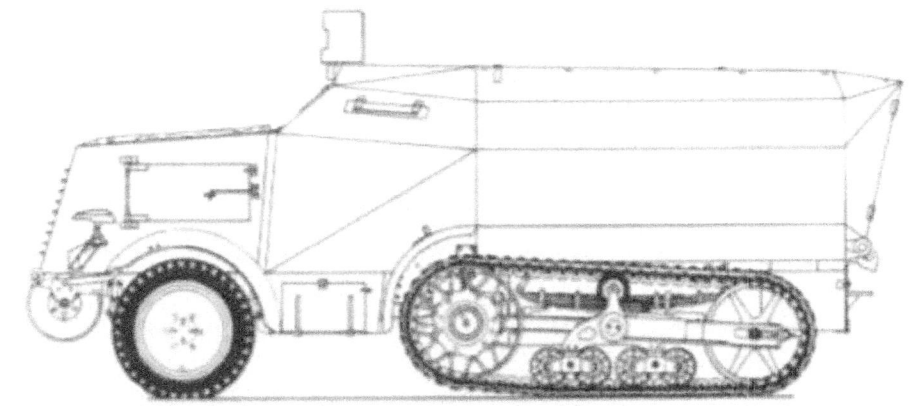

Schutzenpanzer wagen Aufbau geschlossen

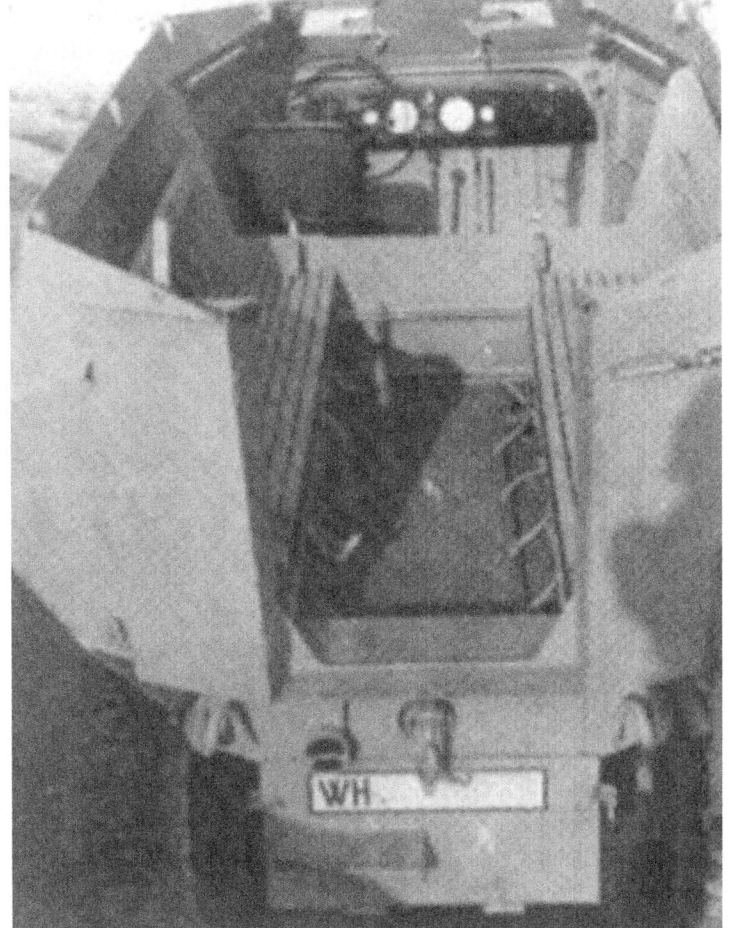

The interior of the personnel carrier version of the UNIC was similar to that of the 251/1, having a wood-slatted bench along each side of the crew compartment, as can be seen in the photo

Armored personnel carrier U304 (f) on the way to the front. Normandy, 1944

Platoon leader armored car with 3.7cm PaK 36

Zugfuhrerwagen mit PaK 36

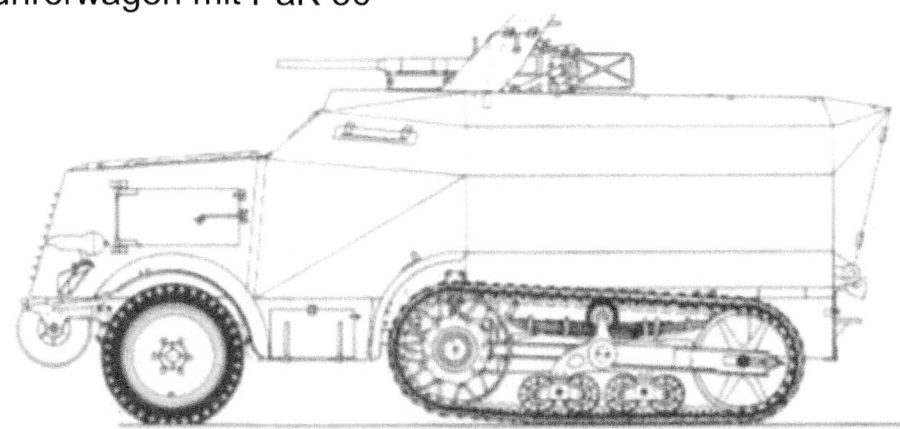

Zugfuhrerwagen mit PaK 36 auf UNIC P 107, Kennnummer U304(f)
The SPWs of the platoon leaders for each of the armored platoons
(with the exception of the Heavy Company and the heavy platoon of
the rest of the armored companies), according to the K.St.Ns of the
time, was armed with a 3.7 cm Pak. There were 3 per (non-heavy)
SPW Company, so 9 per Armored Battalion. Spielberger features a
view of a fresh platoon leader's SPW. Equivalent of the Sdkfz 251/10,
mounting the 37mm PaK 36, note Anti aircraft machine gun mounting.

Nice view of the Zugfuhrer cariant showing the Pak 36, and the MG
pintle

A destroyed Zugfuhrerwagen with 3.7 cm Pak.A civilian åpsing. As noted above, there were 3 per (non-heavy) SPW Company, so 9 per Armored Battalion. Spielberger features a view of a fresh platoon leader's SPW:

Partially armored self propelled Flak gun carriage
- Selbstfahrlafette (teilgepanzert) für 2-cm-Flak 38

The *teilgepanzert* SP Flak gun carriage for the Flak 38 received the smallest amount of conversion, consisting of the addition of a three-part armored shield mounted on the very front protecting the radiator and the fenders. The middle part of this shield had openable metal slats over the radiator and each outside part had a hole cut in it through which the headlights protruded. The engine compartment and hood remained unchanged (unarmored), except that the windshield was covered or replaced by an armored one which was able to fold down but also had observation flaps in them so that they could be driven with the shield up. The bed of the halftrack was replaced by an armored tub in which was mounted the Flak 38.

As with all of the other conversions that were produced by Baukommando Becker, there are photographs of it taken outside of the workshop and/or shortly after delivery to the troops:

The teilgepanzert SP Flak 38 with the windshield up down.

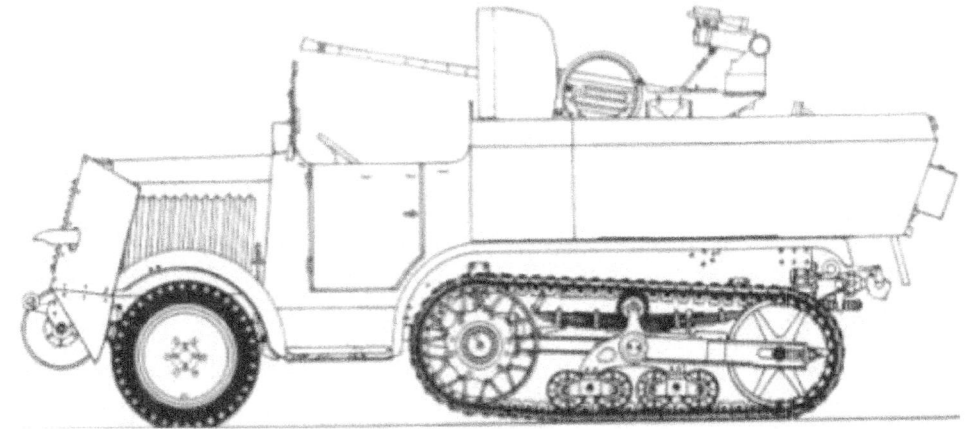

Selbstfahrlafette 2cm FlaK 38(teilgepanzert) auf UNIC P107 Kenn nummer U304(f)

Frontal look of the Selbstfahrlafette 2cm FlaK 38(teilgepanzert) auf
UNIC P107 Kenn nummer U304(f)

A look at he inrerior of the Selbstfahrlafette 2cm FlaK 38(teilgepanzert) auf UNIC P107 Kenn nummer U304(f)
There is a little video of this vehicle on the YouTube channel "Panzer Picture" for those interested.

A battery with half-armored FlaK 38 on the U304 chassis (f) during the development of a combat training task. France, 1943. Selbstfahrlafette U304(f) with FlaK 38. Note driver compartment not armoured

Armored self propelled Flak gun carriage

- Selbstfahrlafette (gepanzert) für 2-cm-Flak 38 (72 Stück bei der Brigade West). 360° Seitenrichtfeld.

The fully armored SP Flak gun carriage for the Flak 38 received a body very similar to the SPW ausf 2 UNIC , but the height of the fighting compartment and the armored cab are cut down so as not to impede the movement and field of fire of the Flak 38.

Self-propelled anti-aircraft anti-aircraft gun based on the U304 (f), equipped with a 20-mm anti-aircraft anti-aircraft system 38. Halftrack tows a trailer with ammunition. (72 produced)

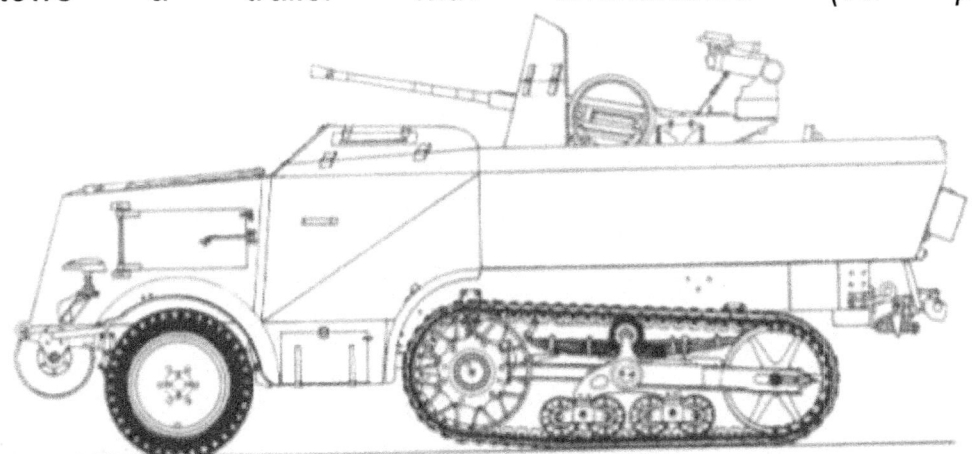

Selbstfahrlafette 2cm FlaK 38(gepanzert) auf UNIC P107 Kenn nummer U304(f)

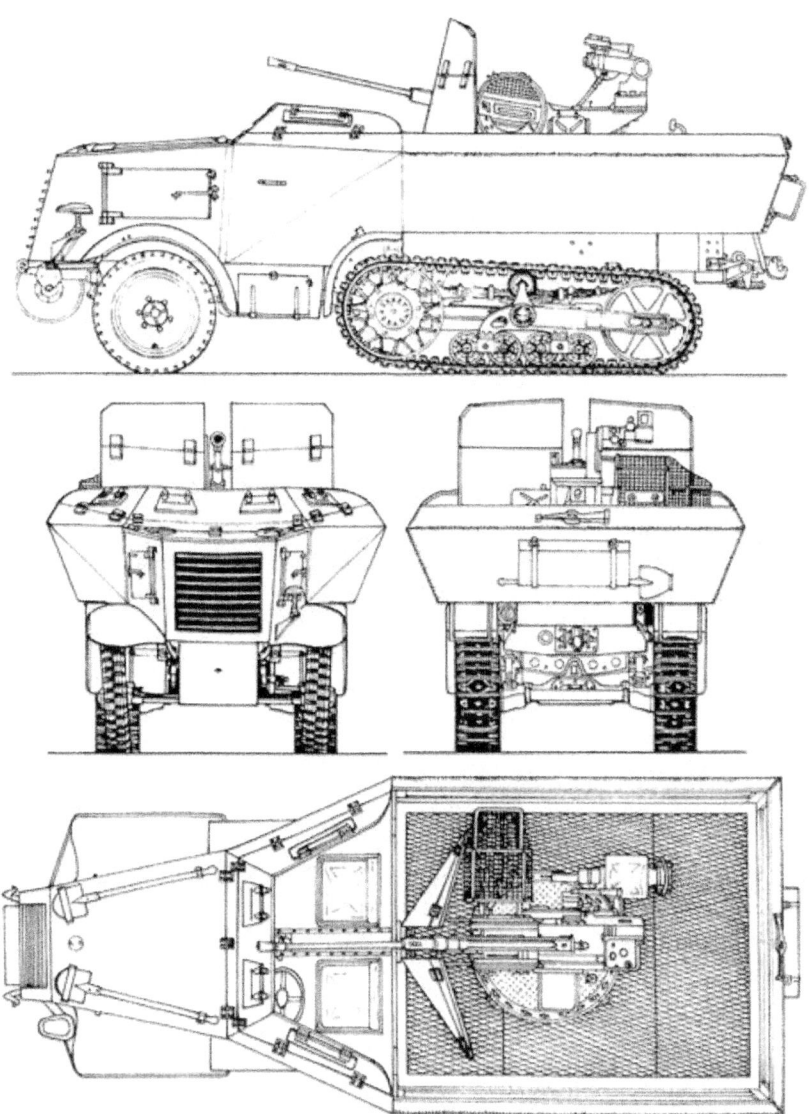

Equivalent of the Sdkfz 251/17, mounting the 20mm Flak 36

Armored Mortar carrier
- Granatwerferpanzer

According to Kortenhaus the heavy platoon of each SPW Company (4th Platoon) was equipped with two of this version of the UNIC . Spielberger lists the *Granatwerferpanzer* as one of the conversions for which Becker used the UNIC as a basis, but no further information nor photos are provided. It is probable that the French Brandt 81mm mortar was employed, just as they were on Somua MCG and MCLs to produce the *Reihenwerfer* versions. There is no known photo of this conversion, or, at least, none in which the mortar is visible.

Armored ambulance

- Sanitätspanzer

There is no documentation of the existence of an armored ambulance version of the UNIC among the records to which I have access. Nonetheless, there is photographic evidence that they were present in Normandy. The SPW Battalion HQ Companies were organized according to K.St.N. 1108 a (gp.) v. 1.4.1943 (a copy of which I have been unable to obtain) but most other K.St.N. for SPW Battalion HQ Companies, such as 1108 a (gp.) dated 1.11.43, authorized 1 mittlerer Krankenpanzerwagen (Sd.Kfz. 251/8). Based on this theoretical organization, each SPW Battalion should have had one UNIC armored ambulance, but could have had more than one.

Armored Radio car

- Funkkraftwagen (gepanzert)

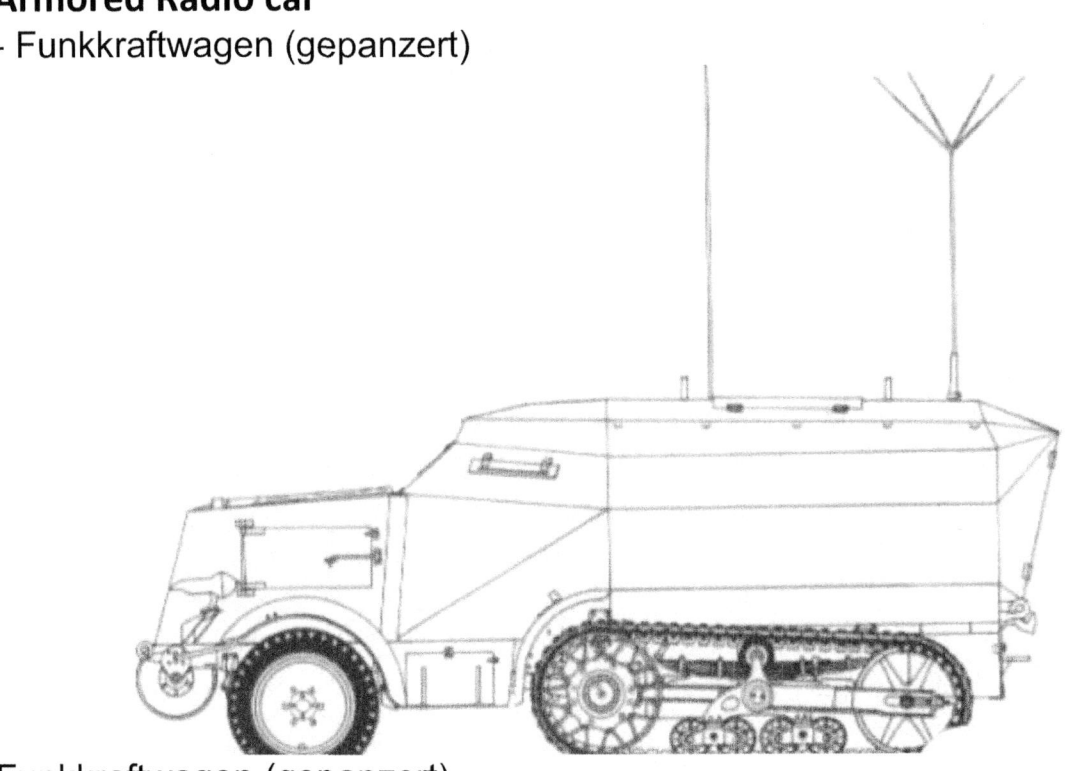

Funkkraftwagen (gepanzert)

leSPW U304(f) (Funk) Nachrichtenkraftwagen, the *equivalent of the Sdkfz 251/3 radio/command vehicles. The internal layout of SPW U 304(f) (Fkl); Note the Jeep on the right*

Based on the numbers, it appears that the *Funkwagen* version of the UNIC was a very common version utilized by 21st Panzer Division.

The radio equipment was stowed in the passenger side rear part of the fighting compartment, following the convention utilized in Sd.Kfz 250 and 251s :

There were, however, some that possibly served also as command vehicles which received a crowned, armored roof in which there were two flaps that allowed access to an MG (notice the pintle). The only known example of this is one that was captured in the Saar region in March 1945.

Funkkraftwagen (gepanzert), note the antennas

The majority of these were probably open topped as shown above

While the location and the unusual insignia would tempt us to assume that this is proof that UNIC s with aufbau were assigned to units other than 21st Panzer, that would be an incorrect assumption. This was, in fact, a UNIC of StuG-Abteilung 200 of 21st Panzer. After Normandy, Stug-Abteilung 200 was removed from 21st Panzer as it was reorganized along a more standard organization. This abteilung was not broken up but rather was transferred. Hans Weber, "The connection is StuG Abt 200 was first with 21. Pz. Div. later under the name of HStuG Brigade 200 in the Ardennes.

There were roughly twice as many UNIC P 107s produced as Somua MCGs and MCLs put together but, ironically, the photographic record of the latter is larger (at least in terms of the armored versions), as we will see in part 2. Nonetheless, the known photographic record of 21st Panzer UNIC's is much larger.

Bibliography

Anonymous. D 628/1 Leichter Zugkraftwagen U (f) Typ P 107: Gerätbeschriebung und Bediennungsanweisung zum Fahrgestell. Berlin, 1941.

Buffetaut, Yves. Les Panzer en Normandie. (Militaria Hors-Série No. 1). Paris: Histoire & Collections, 1991.

Bernage, Georges; Leterreux, Frédéric & Wirton, Phillipe. Le Couloir de la Mort: Falaise-Argentan. Bayeux: Editions Heimdal, 2007. ISBN 2-84048-217- 7.

Bernage, Georges & Wirton, Philippe. Goodwood: Normandy 1944. Bayeux: Editions Heimdal, 2006. ISBN 2-84048-189-8.

Boniface, Jean-Michel & Jeudy, Jean-Gabriel. Scout Cars & Half-Tracks. Paris: Éditions Presse Audiovisuel, 1989. ISBN: 2-85120-316-9.

Cance, Hubert. "L'UNIC P-107, Un Tracteur A Travers La Guerre". Steel Masters: Le Magazine des Blindes et du Modelisme Militaire, No. 39. (Histoire & Collections, Paris, Juin-Juillet, 2000.), Pp 28-32.

Cance, Hubert. "Les UNIC P-107 Blindés Allemands." Steel Masters: Le Magazine des Blindes et du Modelisme Militaire, No. 40. (Histoire & Collections, Paris, Aout-Septembre, 2000.) Pp 26-30.

Chamberlain, Peter & Doyle, H.L. Semi-Tracked Vehicles of the German Army 1939-45, Part 2: Leichter Schuetzenpanzerwagen, Light Armoured Personnel Carriers (SdKfz 250 & Others). Bellona Handbook No. 2. Berkshire: Bellona Publications Ltd., 1970.

Daugherty, Leo. The Battle of the Hedgerows: Bradley's First Army in Normandy, June-July, 1944. Shepperton, Surrey: Ian Allen, 2001. ISBN 0-7110-2832-X.

Fleischer, Wolfgang. Captured Weapons and Equipment of the German Wehrmacht, 1938-1945. Atglen, PA: Schiffer Military History, 1998. ISBN: 0764305263.

Jaugitz, Marcus. Funklenkpanzer: The History of German Army Remote- and Radio-Controlled Armor Units. Alberta: JJ Fedorowicz, 2006. ISBN: 0921991584.

Kortenhaus, Werner. 21. Panzerdivision, 1943-45. Uelzen, Verlag Wolfgang Schneider, 2007. ISBN: 978-3-935107-11-2.

Morgan, Joe. "UNIC -Fication: A Yummy French treat from H&K" Military Miniatures in Review, No. 13. (Ampersand Publishing, Delray Beach, FL, Summer 1997.) Pp. 29-31.

Spielberger, Walter J. Beute-Kraftfahrzeuge und Panzer der Deutschen Wehrmacht. Stuttgart: Motorbuch Verlag, 1989.

Vauvillier, François & Touraine, Jean-Michel. L'Automobile sous l'Uniforme 1939-1940. Paris: Editions Ch. Massin, 1992. ISBN: 2-7072-0197-9.

Zaloga, Steven & Balin. D-Day Tank Warfare: Armoured Combat in the Normandy Campaign June-August, 1944. Hong Kong: Concord Publications Co., 1997. No ISBN

Zaloga, Steven. Panzers in the Gunsights: German AFVs in the ETO 1944-45 in US Army Photos. Hong Kong: Concord Publications Co., 2005. ISBN 962-361-093-9.

Captured & converted French equipments in axis service

Printed in Great Britain
by Amazon

12523688R00066